TWILIGHT GALLERY

NINE SHORT PLAYS FROM THE FIFTH DIMENSION

EXIT INTERVIEW

2AMK9

INGRID AND MARGARET

THE DRILL

ALEX IS

NANCY

YOU SEE DEAD PEOPLE?!

OU TOPOS

FRESH MINT

A Plays to Order collection
Published by Plays To Order
5724 Hollywood Blvd., Suite 109
Los Angeles, CA 90028
www.playstoorder.com

© 2016, 2017 Sean Abley, David Beach, Maura Campbell, Caitlin Gilman, Byron Harris, Nick McCord, Sean Michael McCord, Kimberly Patterson, Meredith Williams Rogan

First Edition: September 2017

ISBN-13: 978-0998417325
ISBN-10: 0998417327

Page to Stage Theatre Company presents:

TWILIGHT GALLERY

**NINE SHORT PLAYS FROM THE FIFTH DIMENSION**

Written by

SEAN ABLEY	DAVID BEACH
MAURA CAMPBELL	CAITLIN GILMAN
BYRON HARRIS	NICK MCCORD
SEAN MICHAEL MCCORD	KIMBERLY PATTERSON

MEREDITH WILLIAMS ROGAN

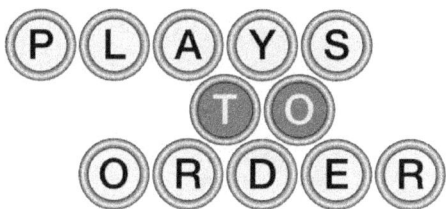

PLAYS TO ORDER

TABLE OF CONTENTS

ABOUT PAGE TO STAGE THEATRE

Page to Stage Theatre Company is a joint venture between a husband and wife team, Nick McCord and Vanessa Mills, that began in the Fall of 2016 in the absence of any New Works theatre production companies in the Roanoke Valley.

McCord, a playwright, had just moved from Seattle to the Roanoke valley for graduate school, and both he and his wife Vanessa, an accomplished actor in her own right, having run small theatre companies in the Pacific Northwest, searched for creative outlets in Southwest Virginia that specialized in New Play Development.

Finding none, they decided to form an LLC, and funded almost the entirety of Page to Stage Theatre's inaugural year from their meager salaries working in social services. Actors, the valley had in spades, and new works, thanks to the Hollins University Playwright's Lab, were ample. Securing a venue was not so easy.

As luck would have it, a local Roanoke high school drama teacher, Les Epstein, volunteered the stage at Community High, and a vibrant partnership was formed.

With Vanessa Mills at the helm, and Nick McCord as the first Artistic Director, in the first year their small theatre company produced 27 original works to full production, many of which had never even seen a reading.

Currently in their second season (as of this writing), Page to Stage continues to produce new and poignant drama. Mills currently heads an artistic team, consisting of herself, Graham Grasty, Kelly Anglim, and Tatiana Durant.

ABOUT TWILIGHT GALLERY

The Twilight Gallery, a portmanteau of Rod Serling's *Twilight Zone* and its 1980s sister *Night Gallery,* was a New Works collection of 1950s-style thrillers commissioned by Nick McCord for inclusion in a Halloween showcase in October 2016.

Divided into two episodes and playing over two weekends, the plays, like Serling's programs before, ranged in theme from limbo-borne existentialism to spectral canines that attack nasty landlords. Ryan Nakamoto provided lighting design, Nick McCord, sound design, and varying local directors lent their expertise in orchestrating what could only be a nightmarishly complicated piece of theatre.

Still, the show was a great success, and, as the inaugural showcase for Roanoke's Page to Stage Theatre, it set a fevered tempo for the young production company. It was a strange, fast-paced time for actor, writer, director and technician alike, and likely, one we won't ever forget.

So we invite you to sit back and enjoy this collection of spooky tales, and poignant allegories—in a different time, a different space... neeny neeny. Neeny neeny.

Page to Stage Theatre

ACKNOWLEDGEMENTS

Exit Interview, 2AMK9, Ingrid and Margaret, The Drill, Alex Is, Nancy, You See Dead People?!, Ou Topos and *Fresh Mint* were produced collectively on October 21st and 22nd, 2016 as *Twilight Gallery* by Page To Stage Theatre Company, Roanoke, VA. The production was directed by: Graham Grasty, Stevie Holcomb, Michael Mansfield, Nick McCord and Vanessa Mills. The cast included: Kelly Anglim, Deena Booth Sasser, Tatiana Durant, Graham Grasty, Jan Hodnett, Caroline King, Erica Musyt, Thom Moore, Patrick Regal, Rachel Sailer and Hunter Wilson.

Exit Interview was first performed as part of Locally Sourced: Original Works from the Live Arts Playwright's Lab, August 2016. The production was directed by Kate Adamson and produced by Scott Dunn. The cast was as follows:

Philip Lawton	Interviewer
Lisa Weigold	Interviewee
Arthur McCord	Construction Worker

Exit Interview was next produced as part of We All (Still) Make Mistakes, The B Sides: A Drunken Mixtape by Sundown Collaborative Theatre, Sept./Oct. 2016. The production was directed by Nolan Chapa and produced by Chloe McDowell. The cast was as follows:

Daniel Adam Bryant-Gawne	Interviewer
Lindsey Hall	Interviewee
Robert Linder	Construction Worker

Fresh Mint was first presented in a staged reading as part of Pacific Play Company's Urban Legends Festival in 2015. Directed by Jen Moon. The cast was as follows:

Erin Ison	Jenny
Susan Echols-Orton	Man

TWILIGHT GALLERY

INTRODUCTION

If the *Twilight Gallery* collection is performed as one evening of theater, this optional introduction to the entire evening may be used.

(*HOST enters in a suit. He is serious. Seriously.*)

HOST. Ladies and gentlemen, allow yourselves for a moment, to be teleported back to a dimension in time, a region in space– vast, and perilous, between waking and dreams, the intersection of science and superstition, and, for our purposes, legally dissimilar to any pre–existing licenses or copyright. I mean, come on.

Tonight, the [NAME OF THEATER] would like to present you an offering– a talisman, if you will, transporting the willing to another world– a world double–parked in the poorly lined space between surety and fear– a curio shop on the seldom trafficked strip mall of the shadowland, we call:

The Twilight Gallery.

EXIT INTERVIEW

By Byron Harris

PLAYWRIGHT'S BIO

BYRON HARRIS is an ex-Fireman, ex-Banker, ex-Bosun's mate on a Cruise Ship, ex-Assignment Editor at the CNN National Desk (for well over a decade), ex-Teacher, and an ex-Bookseller. He is currently pursuing his M.F.A. in playwriting as a member of the Playwright's Lab at Hollins University.

SYNOPSIS

People get let go all the time and one shouldn't take it so personally.

A summons to a hitherto unknown room in the company building leads to an exit interview where everything and nothing seems to matter. And the key to coping centers on snapping beans.

CHARACTERS

THE INTERVIEWER (m)   Older man, compassionate, well-meaning.

THE INTERVIEWEE (f)   20s, professional yet crushed.

INTERVIEWEE #2 (m/f)   Twenty-ish construction worker

SETTING

A room in a wing of the building, previously unknown, somewhere.

PROPS

A table, two chairs, two bowls, a really large pile of string beans, a hard-hat.

EXIT INTERVIEW

By Byron Harris

(*The INTERVIEWER sits alone on the left side of the rectangular table situated center stage. There is an empty chair on the other side of the table. Before him, there is a very large pile of green beans and two bowls, one large and one small. Beginning in darkness and as the lights rise, the INTERVIEWER snaps the beans. The ends go in the small bowl with some string and the green beans themselves go in the large bowl. He's methodical, but not slow with this work. The INTERVIEWEE, dressed in standard professional businesswoman attire, steps tentatively into the room from stage right, clearly not sure if she should be there.*)

HOST. Picture if you will a normal day at work, full of frenzy and tedium, busy with duties and droning co-workers, hard sets of urgencies of one sort or another rise and fall. You are walking down a familiar hallway, your head full of things that need doing as you take an unthinking turn and find yourself out of joint, out of time facing a man at a table snapping a massive pile of green beans…

(*HOST exits.*)

INTERVIEWEE. Excuse me?
INTERVIEWER. Yes.
INTERVIEWEE. I was told to come here.
INTERVIEWER. Then come in. Have a seat. Please.

(*The INTERVIEWEE stands uncertainly as INTERVIEWER keeps snapping beans.*)

INTERVIEWEE. Not really sure why I need to be here. We're on deadline with Project Tarzan. My team's knee deep in code and I need to grapple with things. (*Beat.*) If it's just the same to you, I'd like to get back to them, pronto. We don't really have time. (*Beat.*) So I'll be leaving now if that's ok?

INTERVIEWER. If you need to go, by all means feel free to go. Don't let me hold you up.

INTERVIEWEE. Thank you, that's kind. (*Beat.*) Alright, I'll see you around...

(*INTERVIEWEE exits stage right. INTERVIEWER continues snapping beans. After a five count, she returns from right.*)

INTERVIEWEE. I seem to be going in circles. Do you know how to get back to the main workspace? I've never been in this part of the building before.

INTERVIEWER. Don't know my way around either. Not really. Have a seat, no?

(*The INTERVIEWEE sits back in empty chair.*)

INTERVIEWEE. I want to be back with my team. I know this project backwards and forwards and I need to be supervising their work, especially now. I'm not sure why I'm here at all.

INTERVIEWER. I'm sure you're essential. But since you're here already, sit a spell. Who are you?

INTERVIEWEE. I'm a Project Coordinator in New Products. I report to Ted Hensley, Vice President and Director of New Products. And I would like to speak to him now. Right this minute as a matter of fact.

INTERVIEWER. Miss, I'm sure you have a lot of concerns and questions about everything. But I can't put you in touch with this Mr. Hensley.

INTERVIEWEE. Just who are you? Do you have a name sir...

INTERVIEWER. Yes, of course.

INTERVIEWEE. Then tell me who you think you are putting me here in... some dungeon when I've important work to be doing that matters a great deal toward this company's reputation and the bottom line. Name, now!?!

(*The INTERVIEWER for the first time pauses snapping the beans, thinks for a beat before responding with energy. He resumes snapping.*)

INTERVIEWER. My name's not important. I mean it's materially insignificant. And you shouldn't be worrying about things like that. What I'm trying to say is your job, this project... Apeman or whatever shouldn't be weighing on you so much. At all really.

INTERVIEWEE. Project Tarzan, bozo. It could send the stock swirling to new heights. It may revolutionize the point of sale industry. It's my path up the food chain.

INTERVIEWER. But it's really not your concern, not anymore at least. I can say with absolute certainty that the project'll be finished, just without your participation.

INTERVIEWEE. Are you saying I'm being let go? You're firing me?

INTERVIEWER. What I'm saying is that you should start focusing on the big picture. There are things that you care about, people you care about. This might be a good time for reflection.

INTERVIEWEE. That tool Hensley.

INTERVIEWER. Excuse me?

INTERVIEWEE. I told Teddy "Ladies Man" Hensely that we'd fallen behind, but we'd licked it. We're going to make first of the month with room to spare. So the spazoid freaks and panic-fires me. He'll oversee things and roll in glory as my team crosses the finish line.

INTERVIEWER. Well, I don't know the man, but that sounds pretty under-handed. I'm sure...

INTERVIEWEE. I'm sure the goof's already booking his Hawaiian trip. Probably on Orbitz right now snagging two first class tickets for him and Emma from Marketing. You let the man paw you twice a week, you live in one world. Swat the filthy hand away, you live in another.

INTERVIEWER. Sounds like a terrible place to work...

INTERVIEWEE. I like it though. I rose even though I didn't do the Ted lap-dance. You see, if you're competent, you got a place, a perch. So I made myself indispensable so this wouldn't happen. This shouldn't be happening. You need to write this down. I'm dishing here.

INTERVIEWER. As I said earlier, none of this really amounts to a hill of beans.

(*They both look at the pile of beans on the table.*)

INTERVIEWEE. So to speak. (*Beat.*) The hell it doesn't. That's a grade A felony, sexual harassment dead-to-rights. If he takes me down over Tarzan, which I was in the process of saving damn it to hell, then I'm singing like a canary. Write this down HR man.

INTERVIEWER. I don't work in HR. I don't, really.

INTERVIEWEE. HR types like to lie low, building paper trails. But the gophers do come out of their holes for the executions. Why do they call it "human resources" anyhow? So they can drain us dry I tell you. I'm a human being, not a commodity you, you rodent!

INTERVIEWER. Exactly! My advice: seize your humanity! Expand your horizons. Grow.

INTERVIEWEE. Good thoughts HR Chimp. See now that you're firing me, I can say things like that. And I'll call you a bonehead loser all day long since you refuse to write down my story. That Teddy always walks. Got some upstairs juice that keeps him clean. By the bye, what are the terms?

INTERVIEWER. Excuse me?

INTERVIEWEE. Where are my walking papers? Don't you have a packet with my severance, some lame pamphlet on getting counseling, like I can afford it now. Just so you have no liability if I go home and slit my wrists. I'm sure the folder's about here somewhere....

(*INTERVIEWEE looks around, picks up a handful of beans, they spill out, drops pile.*)

INTERVIEWER. There's no packet, at least that I'm aware of.

INTERVIEWEE. And my things? My plant, my mug. You know, my shit. Where's the box?

INTERVIEWER. I've no idea honestly.

INTERVIEWEE. What kind of an HR clown are you? I'm already leaving here to go straight to a lawyer, but you're going make this too easy. This is so screwed up, you might as well start packing up your own desk. What a crappy company this turned out to be.

INTERVIEWER. I don't work for your company.

(*They look at each other. They look at the beans.*)

INTERVIEWEE. So you're supposed to be some imported, cool as a cucumber contract worker who jets in from nowhere, lays off a hundred of us, then flies back to nowhere. I saw the movie. Well, if that's the case, you suck. They're not getting their money's worth with your sorry ass. What's with the beans anyway?

INTERVIEWER. They seem to help.

INTERVIEWEE. The hell they do. They're not helping at all.

INTERVIEWER. Most people don't take five seconds to think through the string bean. If they get told by someone to go snap, they go watch TV and rip willy-nilly. But there's an art to it, there really is. First, you need to snap when you snap. No screwing around, you really got to pop the thing. You got to hear it snap. And you only need to do one end, the end that grew on the vine. You need supple fingers to do the next bit, that is pull down gently; you'll draw the string out slowly away from the pod. You know, there are two strings, but usually only one's developed enough to bother with. If it tears, try the other end.

INTERVIEWEE. What do your damned string beans have to do with me getting fired today?

INTERVIEWER. Nothing.

INTERVIEWEE. Nothing?

INTERVIEWER. Nothing.

INTERVIEWEE. Then why am I here?

INTERVIEWER. Now that's a good question. Why are we here?

INTERVIEWEE. I asked you. I got sent here. I want to leave.

INTERVIEWER. Then leave. Nothing's stopping you.

(*INTERVIEWEE rises to leave then sits back down.*)

INTERVIEWEE. It's all so pointless. You see I'm good at my job. This is really unexpected. Surprising. Disappointing.

INTERVIEWER. You married?

INTERVIEWEE. Dating. His name's Augie. (*Beat.*) Augie's a nice guy.

INTERVIEWER. Siblings?

INTERVIEWEE. An older sister who runs a weavery in New Zealand and never visits.

INTERVIEWER. Parents still living?

INTERVIEWEE. Yeah, both of them. They got a place outside of Fresno. Nice house. I get up there now and again. Not enough really. What about you?

INTERVIEWER. Two grand-kids: Obadiah and Ophelia. My daughter has a thing for Os. Married this slacker roofer dude that hates me. She works in a tank factory in Lima. Builds turrets for M1 Abrams. Thirty-five and already running a line. (*Beat.*) I had a son too. Don't know much about him.

(*INTERVIEWEE picks up a bean and slowly starts to snap one. Then another and another [and so on].*)

INTERVIEWER. If you like, I'll tell you three cringe moments in my life... you know those moments you'd take back if you could.

INTERVIEWEE. Cringe moments? Can this get weirder? Sure, spill...

(*Both snap beans with alacrity and precision.*)

INTERVIEWER. In fourth grade, three of us set a fire to a pile of leaves outside this empty barn... barn went up in flames of course. No one knew and no one got hurt, but turned out the owner used the place to store antique doors. I remember walking through the ashes and tripping over all these cast-iron door knobs. (*Beat.*) I was a young lawyer, won a case, but the judge ritually humiliated me at every pass. Went for groceries afterwards, just grabbing the basics after a long day and this kid starts bagging all wrong, eggs on bottom and all that. I start busting his chops, like flat-out screaming at him and I look up; he's this retarded, I'm sorry this mentally challenged dope. Hated myself for that. (*Beat.*) My wife, she left me for another lawyer. Just a single-shingle guy, not even a name firm. They were together, laughing over coffee. I saw her and she saw I saw. Stood on the balls of my feet, then walked away. Had to be in court. Never brought it up. The whole sorry saga of my divorce went on from there.

INTERVIEWEE. Ok, now suppose I don't feel like sharing. Not sure about the group hug thing.

INTERVIEWER. Then just snap beans. It helps... You get used to things.

INTERVIEWEE. Where did the beans come from?

(*They look at each other, snapping all the while.*)

INTERVIEWER. They were just here. When I arrived the little girl showed me how to snap.

INTERVIEWEE. Who?

INTERVIEWER. The little girl. Talked to me. Taught me about the beans. Snapped with me.

INTERVIEWEE. What did this little girl say?

INTERVIEWER. Said to stay as long as it took. And to keep snapping. Then she left.

INTERVIEWEE. Where did she go?

INTERVIEWER. Away. Somewhere.

INTERVIEWEE. Where's somewhere? Where's away?

INTERVIEWER. I don't really know. Just went away. (*Beat.*) Left me here to snap the beans.

INTERVIEWEE. Cause it helps. How does it help you?

INTERVIEWER. Helps me not to think about Maggie with my O-boy and my O-girl. Might as well be raising them by herself. About missing Obadiah on the baseball field cause he had some- thing when he pitched. Cocky kid, but he can bring some heat. And Ophelia can play the oboe to make the stones weep.

INTERVIEWEE. You can still go see them right?

INTERVIEWER. I don't think so. You see before I came here I remember being on an elevator; our firm's on the 29th floor. I remember pressing the button and leaning up against the wall, just sliding backwards. My chest hurt. There was this lady shaking me...

INTERVIEWEE. This isn't about my job is it?

INTERVIEWER. No, it's not. I tried to tell you that your work, my work, well they just don't matter anymore. Do you remember anything about how you came here?

INTERVIEWEE. Raoul and I were reviewing code on his laptop. I saw this flash and heard this loud noise— that's all I remember. Wait, there was heat... and my head....

(*INTERVIEWEE stops snapping suddenly. The INTERVIEWER continues to snap.*)

INTERVIEWER. Keep snapping.

(*INTERVIEWEE looks at him in shock.*)

INTERVIEWER. Snap I say. Snap! Snap! Snap!

(*INTERVIEWEE renews snapping with vigor.*)

INTERVIEWEE. Made out with Mike Johansson from IT. Just for the hell of it. Never told Augie. (*Beat.*) Hid my stash of pot in my sister's room and when Mom found it I played dumb. Let her take the rap. (*Beat.*) I've three DWIs and the state's suspended my license... I still drive.
INTERVIEWER. Thank you.
INTERVIEWEE. This does help.
INTERVIEWER. I think I need to go. I feel like I… Been good to get to know you a bit.
INTERVIEWEE. Thank you for being kind.
INTERVIEWER. Of course. Keep snapping and all that.

(*The INTERVIEWER rises, gestures farewell, turns around, then exits. INTERVIEWEE snaps beans relentlessly for a five count. A new INTERVIEWEE, a construction worker, enters.*)

INTERVIEWEE #2. I was told to come here.

(*INTERVIEWEE looks up with compassion, still snapping. In that instant, she realizes she is now the INTERVIEWER.*)

INTERVIEWER. Have a seat then.
INTERVIEWEE #2. Don't mind if I do. Take a load off. Good to get off the site. (*Beat.*) I hate to ask, but what's with the beans?

END OF PLAY

2AMK9

By Kimberly Patterson

PLAYWRIGHT'S BIO

KIMBERLY PATTERSON spent more than a decade in New York City working in Off- and Off-Off Broadway theaters in almost every capacity possible. As a playwright, her plays have appeared in the New York International Fringe Festival, the Orlando Fringe Festival, and the New York Musical Theater Festival; her musical, *Oedipus for Kids!*, is published by Samuel French and has been produced around the U.S. and in Canada. *Douchenozzle,* her latest musical, was workshopped in Nashville and premiered at Orlando Fringe in 2017. Based in South Florida, Kimberly was a participant in the 2017 New Play Festival with Theatre Lab at FAU and is a regular 1MPF playwright. She is a member of the Playwright's Lab at Hollins University and the Dramatists Guild.

SYNOPSIS

Good dog.

Every night, Janice is visited by a dog that only she can see. Is she going crazy, or is the dog there to see her?

CHARACTERS

JANICE (f)

Early 20s. Recent transplant from the big city—she clearly is looking for somewhere safe to rest, and if her insomnia is any indication, she's having trouble finding it.

LANDLORD (m)

Mid 30-40s. The epitome of macho sleaze. Stands too close, makes too many small touching gestures. His physical presence should be considerably large. His name is Ray.

VIVIAN (f)

Mid-late 60s. The chatty, happy neighbor.

BENNY (m)

Mid-late 60s. Vivian's more sedate husband.

SETTING

The American suburbs.

PRODUCTION NOTES

The dog is a shadow puppet. Shadow puppets are fun and easy to make! Cut out the preferred shape of dog from a piece of rigid card stock. Attach it to a thin wooden dowel. When the puppet is placed against a sheer white fabric and lit from behind, we see it as a shadow image on the fabric. If you are very crafty, you can make fully articulated puppets by cutting out limbs separately (or a tail) and attaching them at joint locations with brass brads. Screens can be as simple as a lightweight white fabric with a flashlight/utility light for the illumination.

2AMK9

By Kimberly Patterson

HOST. Janice moved to the suburbs in search of life at a slower pace. But the quiet solitude isn't as calming as she'd hoped. Perhaps she could get herself a nice, friendly dog for company? Unfortunately, her landlord has a firm "no pets" policy—and a loose grasp of right and wrong. So Janice can't have a dog, but maybe a dog could have *her*, since her new neighborhood is in The Twilight Gallery.

(*HOST exits.*)

Scene One

(*The stage contains a plain backyard and a white screen. A soundscape in the dark: city noises of cars, buses, and other urban traffic give way to crickets, soft wind in trees and bushes. JANICE enters with the LANDLORD.*)

LANDLORD. I think you'll like it here. Great neighborhood. Quiet.
JANICE. Quiet is good.
LANDLORD. It's kinda a fixer–upper, but you said you like to work with your hands?
JANICE. I'm happier when I have a project.
LANDLORD. I'm happy to come help you with anything... anything at all. You've got my personal cell number. Feel free to use it any time, day or night. So, whaddya say?
JANICE. Okay. Do I sign something now?

(*THE LANDLORD gives her a packet of papers and a pen, and leans forward so she can use his back to write on. When the transaction is complete, he hands her the keys.*)

LANDLORD. Welcome home.

(*He exits. After surveying the yard, JANICE exits.*)

Scene Two

(*Evening. The shadow puppet dog appears from behind the screen. Sounds: snuffling, sniffing, the rustling of branches and bushes, the jangle of its collar. JANICE enters and sees the dog as if from a window.*)

JANICE. (*To the dog.*) It's 2 AM. I am wide awake. It is *too* quiet. What are you doing up?

(*She watches the dog until it fades, then exits.*)

Scene Three

(*Morning. The backyard. JANICE is raking. VIVIAN enters.*)

VIVIAN. Well, hi there!
JANICE. Hello.
VIVIAN. I'm Vivian. Welcome to the neighborhood!
JANICE. Janice. Thanks.
VIVIAN. Are you settling in ok?
JANICE. Yeah, so far / everything is fine.
VIVIAN. (*Calling offstage.*) Benny! Benny, come meet the new neighbor.
BENNY. Hiya.
JANICE. Hello / I'm Janice.
VIVIAN. Janice just moved in.
BENNY. You come up from the city?
JANICE. Yeah.
VIVIAN. It's nice here. Quiet.
JANICE. That's what everyone says.
VIVIAN. You'll get used to it.
BENNY. And don't you mind Ray. He likes it when pretty girls rent the place, but shouldn't have anything to worry about. His wife keeps him on a tight leash.
JANICE. That's... comforting.
VIVIAN. You just let us know if you need anything.
JANICE. Oh, hey... I saw a dog in the yard last night?
VIVIAN. What's that?

JANICE. A brownish dog, sort of medium size? In the backyard. Does it belong to someone?

VIVIAN. Benny, you know of anyone around here with dogs?

BENNY. Dogs, you say? Hm.

JANICE. Just the one dog. I didn't know if I should tell someone it got out, or something?

BENNY. Nobody 'round here has any I know of. Stray?

JANICE. I don't think so... he had a collar.

BENNY. There are some migrant workers that camp out in the field behind Winn–Dixie. I've seen them with dogs / sometimes.

VIVIAN. Then it's probably a Mexican dog! Or Salvadorian!

BENNY. Doesn't sound like something you need to worry about.

VIVIAN. Say you'll come have dinner with us tomorrow night!

JANICE. Um.

VIVIAN. Oh, wonderful! Around 6:30?

JANICE. Ok?

VIVIAN. Fantastic! Ta–ta!

(*VIVIAN and BENNY exit.*)

JANICE. Wow. Ok.

(*JANICE continues raking until the lights change to night.*)

Scene Four

(*Night. JANICE looks again from her window. The shadow dog returns. She talks to it.*)

JANICE. You come here every night. Always after midnight. I know because I still Do Not Sleep. I can tell when you're coming because your chain. It makes noise. Are you out there watching me back?

(*JANICE exits. The shadow dog romps against the screen. Sound: rain. His chain jangling mixes with the sound of rain. Then the shadow dog fades.*)

Scene Five

(*Morning. The rain has stopped during the night. THE LANDLORD enters. He peers around the yard for a few moments until JANICE enters.*)

LANDLORD. I'm glad I caught you.

JANICE. Is something wrong?

LANDLORD. Of course not. You never called me, so I thought I'd come by, see if you have everything you need. Maybe something I could take care of for you.

JANICE. No. Thanks. / I'm good.

LANDLORD. Backyard starting to look good.

JANICE. I'm working on it.

LANDLORD. Come on down here, I wanna show you the property line. Don't want you to dig up someone else's yard on accident.

JANICE. It rained last night.

LANDLORD. Sure did. Come take a look.

(*She approaches, but is then distracted by the surroundings.*)

JANICE. There aren't any prints. Everything is muddy, but no sign of paw prints.

LANDLORD. Something getting into your garden?

JANICE. I think there's been a dog... maybe someone's work dog got out?

LANDLORD. Oh, the migrant camp. Well, season's almost over. They'll be moving on.

JANICE. I don't know if I should call someone.

LANDLORD. I'll look into it. Now. This property line. Come closer — I don't bite.

JANICE. I'm good over here.

LANDLORD. See a little stone marker. See that?

JANICE. Yeah.

LANDLORD. So the property line... are you sure you can see / where I'm pointing?

(*He puts his hands on her, ostensibly to move her to a better vantage point.*)

JANICE. (*Stepping quickly away from him.*) I can see.

LANDLORD. Yeah, the marker. Property line. Very important. There are all sorts of rules, and I'd hate for you to break one. It means your lease could be terminated.

JANICE. Sorry, have I done something wrong?

LANDLORD. I'm here to help you. But you gotta call me, let me know what's going on. I could come over again, make sure it's all good. You know what I mean?

JANICE. If I think of anything—

LANDLORD. You really need to get in touch.

(*He gives her an appraising look, and then goes off. Repulsed, JANICE stomps down the ground where the marker is. She continues to search the rest of the yard for paw prints and finds none.*)

Scene Six

(*Later on—nighttime. Outside of JANICE's house. JANICE, BENNY and VIVIAN enter.*)

VIVIAN. What a beautiful night! No more rain.

JANICE. You don't need to walk me home.

BENNY. Don't be ridiculous! Happy to do it!

VIVIAN. We saw Ray come around this morning.

JANICE. Something about the property line?

BENNY We're keeping an eye out, don't worry.

JANICE. Am I supposed to / worry?

VIVIAN. Now Benny, don't go frightening the girl.

JANICE. Are you sure no one around here has a dog?

VIVIAN. I did ask around... Mrs. Bethany over of Trinity Road has a Pomeranian. Could that be it?

JANICE. I doubt it.

BENNY. Ok, my dear. Here you are.

JANICE. Dinner was delicious. Thank you.

VIVIAN. No trouble at all.

BENNY. You have any problems at all, you know where we are. If you holler, we can hear you and will come running.

JANICE. Thanks.

VIVIAN. That's what good neighbors are for, dear.

(*The couple exits. Sound: a faint jangling, far away. JANICE looks towards the sound, but nothing appears.*)

Scene Seven

(*Much later. The shadow dog is back. JANICE talks to it.*)

JANICE. The phone's rung three times tonight. I know someone's there: I hear the breathing. I didn't answer after the first one. Now that it's stopped, it's too quiet. You don't think there's something in the bushes? You don't hear that? If *you* don't, it must be nothing. Promise you'll stay here tonight? Outside my window? All I want to do is try to go to sleep. Stay? Stay. Good dog.

(*She exits. The shadow dog remains. Sound: the rustling in the bushes is real, and grows louder. His shadow grows larger. Soft cursing and heavy breathing: It's the LANDLORD, entering with binoculars. He focuses his binoculars on a spot, and watches for a moment. Then he fishes his keys from his pocket and moves in the direction of the house. He hears a dog growl.*)

LANDLORD. (*Looking around, but seeing nothing.*) What the hell?

(*The shadow dog growls again, a warning. Its shadow grows larger.*)

LANDLORD. I know you're out there. Go on, git.

(*The dog snarls and lunges for him. Everything goes dark, but we hear the sounds of the attack. It's loud: snarling dog, a man shouting in pain. JANICE enters, frantic, looks towards the screen, the yard, but there's nothing at all to see. She leaves.*)

Scene Eight

(*Morning. JANICE returns to the backyard, searching for any remnants of the fight she heard last night. Nothing: the lawn is clear and undisturbed.*)

JANICE. (*Calling off.*) Benny? Benny, are you over there?

BENNY. (*Entering.*) Hey there, was just coming by. Vivian's been baking all morning, and she told me to bring you some of her fresh bread. Here you are.

JANICE. Thanks. Hey, did you hear anything last night? Sounded like a dog fight or something?

BENNY. Nothing at all, but I sleep like a rock. Lemme ask Viv. (*Calling off.*) Vivie, come on out of that kitchen for a minute.

VIVIAN. (*Entering.*) What are you going on about? Did you bring her the bread?

JANICE. Yes, thank you.

BENNY. She wants to know if you heard some sort of ruckus last night?

JANICE. Around 2 AM maybe?

VIVIAN. No, there was nothing. I'm sure I would've woken up if I heard it.

JANICE. Weird.

VIVIAN. Having some bad dreams?

(*RAY enters. He's a mess: his hand is bandaged, his face is scratched, and he limps.*)

LANDLORD. There's a strict no–pets policy.

JANICE. I don't have any pets.

LANDLORD. You're lying. You have a dog.

JANICE. I swear, I don't.

LANDLORD. I can go in, search the apartment. It's my property.

JANICE. Go ahead. I don't have any pets.

VIVIAN. It's true. If she'd had a dog, we'd've noticed. I'm a busybody.

BENNY. She is.

LANDLORD. I can have you evicted. You let that dog get at me. I know you were there, and you didn't do a thing to stop it.

JANICE. Did you call me last night?

BENNY. You have an accident, Ray? Looks like you're in bad shape.

LANDLORD. I'm going to search for that damn dog, and I'm going to have it killed.

JANICE. What did the dog look like?

LANDLORD. I don't know.

VIVIAN. It wasn't invisible.

BENNY. How can you not know?

LANDLORD. It was dark. I couldn't see it.

VIVIAN. You got attacked by an invisible dog?

LANDLORD. It was a real damn dog. It was big. I just couldn't see it very well.

VIVIAN. Raymond, can I get you some water? You don't look well.

LANDLORD. Her dog attacked me last night. I don't know where you're hiding it, but I'm calling animal control, I'm calling the cops.

JANICE. Why were you outside the apartment last night? What were you doing here?

BENNY. Maybe *we* should be calling the cops.

LANDLORD. What are they going to do? This is my property. I'm not trespassing.

JANICE. But *I* could call them. I could tell them that you're making unwanted sexual advances, that I feel uncomfortable. That you keep threatening to evict me. That you make false claims about a dog attack and are here to intimidate me. And the city will care, when I file a claim against you. You'll care when you go to court.

BENNY. We've lived here a long time. We've witnessed a lot of things around this place. A court might like to hear about them. But we didn't hear anything sounding like a dogfight last night.

VIVIAN. Your wife might care. I could call her right now.

JANICE. Maybe she wants to see the property line.

LANDLORD. Hold up. I must've gotten confused with a different property. Clearly you don't have a dog. There's no need for anyone to make any phone calls.

JANICE. If I miss a rent payment, then you can come out here. Otherwise, write me a letter. Don't show up without an appointment. Don't call me.

BENNY. And if she needs any help around the house, she can start with us.

JANICE. Leave now.

LANDLORD. I'm still calling animal control. Damn strays.

(*RAY exits.*)

BENNY. I don't guess a Pomeranian could do *that* to a man.

VIVIAN. I just can't believe I slept through the whole thing. He deserves every single stitch. Now I have an oven to get back to.

BENNY. Like I said, holler if you need anything.

JANICE. Thanks.

(*They exit. JANICE walks around the backyard, inspecting again for signs of a struggle. In the distance, the faint jangling of the chain on a dog's collar.*)

JANICE. Good dog.

END OF PLAY

INGRID
AND
MARGARET

By Sean Abley

PLAYWRIGHT'S BIO

SEAN ABLEY is an award-winning playwright, screenwriter and journalist. He has over thirty plays published by Playscripts, Brooklyn Publishers, Heuer Publishing, Next Stage Press, and Eldridge Plays and Musicals with titles like *End of the World (With Prom to Follow)*, *The Adventures of Rose Red (Snow White's Less-Famous Sister)*, *Horror High: The Musical* and *Attack of the Killer B's*. His play *Popcorn Girl* took 2nd place in the National Partners of the American Theatre Award at the Kennedy Center American College Theatre Festival, and his play *Absence Makes the Heart...* was a national finalist for the John Cauble Short Play contest at the same festival. His television writing includes multiple episodes of *So Weird* (Disney Channel), *Sabrina, the Animated Series* (Disney/UPN), *Digimon* (Fox Family), as well as several pilots including *Bench Pressly, The World's Strongest Private Dick* with Ahmet Zappa. His produced screenplays include the B-movies *Socket, Witchcraft 15: Blood Rose* and *Witchcraft 16: Hollywood Coven*. He was one on the founders of Chicago's prolific Factory Theater in 1992 (still going strong as of this writing), and the creator of the "Gay of the Dead" blog on Fangoria.com.

SYNOPSIS

When the delusion is no longer an illusion, but life...

Henry must decide whether or not to subject his wife, Margaret, to electroshock therapy, sure to cure her multiple personality disorder. But Margaret and Ingrid are resistant—what will happen to the world should Ingrid to disappear?

CHARACTERS

INGRID (f)   A British woman in her 30s who acts as if she's a teenage girl of privilege.

MR. BROWNING (m)   A British butler aged 50s-70s, kindly, has been working for INGRID's family for decades. Will occasionallly slip into impressions of other people flawlessly for INGRID's enjoyment.

HENRY REDDING (m)   A British gentleman aged anywhere from his early 40s to his mid 50s. Firmly middle class. Married to MARGARET.

MARGARET (f)   A British woman in her 30s. She has a pragmatic outlook on life. Married to MR. REDDING.

DOCTOR (m)   A British physician in his 50s.

SETTING

A middle class drawing room in Britain during WWII's Battle of Britain; a doctor's office.

INGRID AND MARGARET

By Sean Abley

Scene One

(*LIGHTS UP on a DRAWING ROOM of the REDDING HOME. This is a modest home of an upper–middle class British family in WWII England. The lighting should suggest a bright morning with many colors rather than a dour, war–ravaged afternoon. There is one entrance, an ornate door to one side or the other. INGRID, a woman in her 30s, dressed a good fifteen years her junior, reads a book, "Tender is the Night" by F. Scott Fitzgerald, while lying on the floor.*)

INGRID. (*Reading aloud.*) "'Think how you love me,' she whispered. 'I don't ask you to love me always like this, but I ask you to remember. Somewhere inside me there'll always be the person I am to–night.'"

(*INGRID clasps the book to her chest and rolls onto her back. We get the sense that she is over dramatic to the core, in the way teenage girls who dream big but live small have perfected, despite the fact she is well into her 30s. But she is not a cloying caricature; in fact she's quite charming in her own way.*)

INGRID. Oh, how I do want to live in an F. Scott Fitzgerald novel! Mr. Browning!

(*MR. BROWNING, a butler, aged anywhere from mid–50s to 70s, enters. He is a kind man, having served INGRID and her family for decades. He treats INGRID as the teenaged girl she presents.*)

MR. BROWNING. Miss Ingrid?
INGRID. I'd like to live in an F. Scott Fitzgerald novel. Wouldn't that be grand?
MR. BROWNING. "The Great Gatsby," miss?
INGRID. Oh, no, Browning. That would be dreary to the core. "Tender is the Night"!

MR. BROWNING. Ah, yes. The story of a young girl—

INGRID. Rosemary!

MR. BROWNING. Rosemary, who goes from being a young actress, to a Hollywood star and the object of unquenchable desire of a married man.

INGRID. Yes! Perfect! Oh, Browning, how can we bring this fantasy to life? Might we send a missive to Mr. Fitzgerald asking permission to enter his beautiful story?

MR. BROWNING. I believe Mr. Fitzgerald has recently died, Miss Ingrid.

INGRID. What? Well, that is terribly inconvenient. Then I propose an alternative. We will create "Tender is the Night" right here, in our drawing room.

MR. BROWNING. Miss Ingrid, preparations must be made for dinner—

INGRID. Oh, shush. If my father gets angry, just refer him to me. There will be no price to pay for your indulgence of his favorite daughter. He can refuse me nothing. Did you know I persuaded him to allow me to stay in this room for a full week just this past May?

MR. BROWNING. I do remember that, miss.

INGRID. My education, for which he paid dearly, has rendered my debate skills irrefutable. "Hoisted on his own petard." That's a phrase I read in a book! I took my meals in here and pretended I was on a ship at sea, miles from land and the comforts of home.

MR. BROWNING. I recall, I was the first mate.

INGRID. Yes! Oh, but now I shall play Rosemary from "Tender is the Night." And you're going to play someone so in love with me, it pains you to avert your eyes from my gaze. Are you ready?

MR. BROWNING. Yes, miss.

INGRID. Do you have a character?

MR. BROWNING. I believe so, miss. I will be a film director.

INGRID. Oh, yes! Rosemary is an actress! And I will be on the set of a film!

MR. BROWNING. Perfect!

INGRID. Alright then, let's begin.

(MR. BROWNING immediately takes on the persona of a Hollywood film director. This impression should be absolute, with

no hesitation or indication MR. BROWNING is for a moment uncomfortable or unprepared for this role.)

MR. BROWNING. (*Film director.*) Rosemary, in this scene you play a young girl, Gilda, who is beautiful, very rich, and has just been thrown from a train.

INGRID. Oh, my!

MR. BROWNING. (*Film director.*) You've rolled down a hill into a pond of quicksand, and you have a sprained ankle.

INGRID. (*Acting.*) Help, I'm sinking! (*As if in pain.*) Ow! Oh, my ankle!

MR. BROWNING. (*Film director.*) Perfect! Now, I've fired the actor hired to play your love interest, because I've fallen in love with you and any attention you receive on or off set will send me into a rage!

INGRID. Oh, goodness!

MR. BROWNING. (*Film director.*) So I will be playing your love interest in the scene. Are you ready to try one?

INGRID. Yes, please! I'm ready for my close up!

(*INGRID drapes herself across a chair, a damaged damsel in repose.*)

MR. BROWNING. (*Film director.*) "The Downward Spiral," Scene One, Take One. Action.

(*SFX: Clapboard clap and SFX: Classic film underscore, their source neither known nor of concern to INGRID or MR. BROWNING.*)

INGRID. (*Acting.*) Oh, help, my love! I'm sinking!

(*MR. BROWNING arrives to save the day.*)

MR. BROWNING. (*Leading man.*) Gilda! Oh, thank goodness you're alright. Let's get you out of this quicksand!

(*MR. BROWNING hefts INGRID off the chair.*)

INGRID. (*Acting.*) Charles, you've saved me from a terrible fate! How may I repay you?
MR. BROWNING. (*Leading man.*) Just love me, Gilda. Love me, won't you?
INGRID. (*Acting.*) I do, Charles, I do!

(*They move in to kiss.*)

MR. BROWNING. (*Film director.*) And cut!
INGRID. Oh, how was that? Did you believe my anguish?
MR. BROWNING. (*Film director.*) Yes, you were perfectly cast as someone who falls into quicksand.
INGRID. Oh, hurrah! Shall we move on to another scene?

(*SFX: Merry–go–round music can be heard from outside.*)

INGRID. Oh! That music! The roundabout!

(*INGRID rushes to the window.*)

INGRID. Oh, I do wish I could see it. It always sounds like it's just around the corner. I imagine it to be colorful and gay. If only I could join the others. Mr. Browning, I have a proposal for you.
MR. BROWNING. Of course, miss.
INGRID. You and I go outside, locate that roundabout, and take it for just one quick spin? Just one?
MR. BROWNING. Apologies, miss. Your father has instructed we should remain indoors for the moment.
INGRID. As always. You would think I was allergic to fresh air with all the time I spend indoors. But no matter. We have our F. Scott Fitzgerald! Shall we play another acting scene?
MR. BROWNING. That will have to wait for another time, miss. Your father asked me to speak to you about Miss Margaret. He'd like you to visit with her today.
INGRID. Oh, no, impossible.
MR. BROWNING. Impossible? But she's just in the next room.
INGRID. Oh, no. Father can't be serious. Tell me he's not.
MR. BROWNING. I'm afraid he is, miss.
INGRID. But Margaret is just awful! Father himself says she's not fit for public consumption. She's castor oil in my tea. She's a

repulsive, terrible mess, skulking about the house. I can't bear the sight of her. I've neither seen nor spoken to her in over a week, and I don't intend to change that today.

MR. BROWNING. Miss Ingrid, your father would ask you take a more charitable view of Miss Margaret.

INGRID. Charitable? How so? Would he like me to give her to the poor? Divide up her body and hand her out to those in need of a good meal? Gladly!

MR. BROWNING. No, miss. He'd like you to be kind to her.

INGRID. Kind? I've avoided her all these years, why start now?

MR. BROWNING. He'd like you to visit her more frequently. To let her join you in the drawing room. Have pity on her. Treat her like family, with pleasant words and activities for two. As your father would rather not expose her to the outside world, only a family member such as yourself could fulfill this position.

INGRID. No, thank you.

MR. BROWNING. Perhaps you could look at the situation as thus—Margaret has spent so long withering on the vine, she's missed the most important moments of a young lady's life. Surely you can see your way to mentoring this girl? Your father realizes it would be a great sacrifice for someone as properly outfitted and beautiful as yourself, but he's hopeful your poise, manners, and confident grasp of the spoken language will be of value to her in some way.

INGRID. Hmmm. Alright then, I'll do it. But no promises! I will visit Miss Margaret and attempt to be cheerful and kind. But if she's too hideous, my charity will end immediately.

MR. BROWNING. Yes, miss.

INGRID. Lead the way. I should squint my eyes, so as to not taint them too quickly with her ugliness.

(INGRID and MR. BROWNING exit. LIGHTS SHIFT to—)

Scene Two

(*DOCTOR'S OFFICE. HENRY REDDING, a gentleman of early 40s–mid 50s in age, speaks with a DOCTOR.*)

HENRY. I'd feel more comfortable having her permission.

DOCTOR. Understood. And women are often capable of making their own decisions when it comes to minor health issues. But can you honestly tell me Margaret's quality of life would be better if she refused this procedure?

HENRY. Of course not.

DOCTOR. As her husband, you've taken an oath before God to protect her health and well–being. Do you still stand by that pledge?

HENRY. Can you explain the procedure again?

DOCTOR. It is very simple. Electrodes are placed on either side of the patient's head, and a rubber guard is placed in their mouth. A burst of electric current is administered, which results in immediate unconsciousness—the patient doesn't feel a thing. The procedure can be administered once, or many times over a period of weeks, depending on the effectiveness of the treatment.

HENRY. It sounds so violent.

DOCTOR. And it can appear to be, as well. The convulsions are unnatural to the untrained eye. And there is the possibility of broken bones from the muscle contractions.

HENRY. Good lord.

(*HENRY paces around the office.*)

HENRY. She's infertile, you know.

DOCTOR. I do.

HENRY. I will be saving my wife to live in a childless marriage. It almost seems cruel on a level.

DOCTOR. But again I ask—what quality of life would Margaret want? What quality of life do you owe her as her husband?

HENRY. And what of Ingrid?

DOCTOR. What of Ingrid? She is irrelevant.

HENRY. As a clinician I understand your dispassionate perspective, but I must say, it's much more difficult for me to just toss her aside than it is for you to tell me to do so.

DOCTOR. Yes, I'm dispassionate. But there is only room for one woman in your household, and it must be the woman you married. It must be Margaret.

HENRY. I understand. I'll speak to her again.

(*LIGHTS SHIFT to—*)

Scene Three

(*DRAWING ROOM. INGRID marches in followed by MR. BROWNING. She turns on him as he enters the room.*)

INGRID. Never again!

MR. BROWNING. Miss Ingrid—

INGRID. Never again! What a terrible woman Margaret is!

MR. BROWNING. If you could remember kindness—

INGRID. I shan't!

MR. BROWNING. –or even pity when it comes to Miss Margaret.

INGRID. Pity? Who should be pitied here? Who, I ask you? That creature is horrid. Filling my head with stories about "the war," and acts of violence so atrocious as not to be believed. To what war does she refer? Hmmm? Is there a war going on outside this window? I see sunlight, and children playing on the street, and old women with groceries and house after beautiful house and not that disgusting panorama of... Oh! My mind is filled with those images!

MR. BROWNING. Your father assures me—

INGRID. My father can rot for all I care! I will not have my precious youth poisoned by that...thing out there.

MR. BROWNING. Miss Ingrid, she's going to have a procedure, and then you'll see. She'll be more to your liking, and then you'll both make your way into society like proper ladies. She'll need your help navigating the rigors of tea dances and introductions to young men—

INGRID. Stop it!

MR. BROWNING. Please, just come out and resume your visit. It would mean so much to your father.

INGRID. I'm not going anywhere near her!

MR. BROWNING. Then I shall bring her in here, at your father's request.

INGRID. You will do no such thing!

(*INGRID produces a key for the door. She quickly locks it.*)

MR. BROWNING. Miss Ingrid, I must insist you unlock that door.

INGRID. I'm not going anywhere, and neither are you!

(*INGRID throws the key out the window.*)

MR. BROWNING. Now see here—

INGRID. No, you see here! That wretched beast will come nowhere near me, today or ever!

HENRY. (*Off.*) Margaret!

INGRID. Who is that?

HENRY. (*Off.*) Margaret? Are you in there?

INGRID. Why is he calling to that beast?

HENRY. (*Off.*) Margaret, I need you to come out here.

INGRID. There's no Margaret in here, and there never will be! Keep that ogress outside!

(*Despite INGRID having locked the door, HENRY opens it easily and enters the drawing room.*)

HENRY. Margaret!

INGRID. She's not in here! Get out!

HENRY. Let me speak to her!

INGRID. No!

HENRY. Ingrid, let me speak to her this instant!

INGRID. I won't!

HENRY. Ingrid...

INGRID. (*Frantic.*) Father, listen to me! Margaret is nowhere within these four walls, nor will she ever be. I couldn't let you speak to her even if I wanted to. Which I don't. Please, father, don't let her corrupt you! Don't let her infect you with her ugliness and that rotting stench! I'll just die if you force her upon me again, I truly will and you will, too!

HENRY. Margaret, I demand you speak to me at once!

(*LIGHTS INSTANTLY CHANGE to—*)

Scene Four

(*A stark, brown and gray palette. The sunny skies have been replaced by clouds. The drawing room is no longer a bright child's room, but a well worn room in a middle–class home. At this point MR. BROWNING enters a pause, not frozen, but no longer a participant in the scene. INGRID is now MARGARET, a woman in her 30s, settled, melancholy.*)

MARGARET. Henry.

HENRY. I'm sorry to shout. It's become the only way to pull you out.

MARGARET. I understand. I'm not angry. You did come into my room, however. We had an agreement.

HENRY. I apologize, but this is our room after all.

MARGARET. Our room indeed.

HENRY. Let's sit down.

(*HENRY and MARGARET sit.*)

HENRY. I spoke to Dr. Corbyn today.

MARGARET. Yes?

HENRY. He remains highly confident of the procedure.

MARGARET. I see.

HENRY. This is good news.

MARGARET. Is it?

HENRY. Margaret...

MARGARET. What if I don't want the procedure?

HENRY. Don't be absurd.

MARGARET. What if I don't?

HENRY. To what end?

MARGARET. To... I don't know. To my end. To my happiness. To my preferred state of being.

HENRY. You're being purposefully enigmatic, but you haven't answered my question.

MARGARET. What is my peace of mind worth to you?

HENRY. I want you to be happy, of course.

MARGARET. But my peace of mind. My day to day... comfort. Is that important?

HENRY. Of course. Aren't you comfortable?

MARGARET. At times.

HENRY. When you're here, present, with me? (*Off her reaction.*) You're not happy?

MARGARET. How could I possibly be?

HENRY. Margaret!

MARGARET. Are you? Are you happy? Be honest with me.

HENRY. It has been a challenge living with your... condition, and if I were being honest, I would have to say that there are times when I'm... less than content. But our happiness is what Dr. Corbyn is advocating. This procedure would eliminate the times of unease, and although our lives wouldn't be perfect—few are—they would certainly less complicated.

MARGARET. I don't believe that to be true.

HENRY. Based on what evidence? Margaret, I say this as kindly as I can, you're a beautiful, intelligent woman, but you're not a doctor.

MARGARET. I say this as kindly as I can—neither are you.

HENRY. But I am your husband, I have a certain level of responsibility for your health.

MARGARET. Yes, my health. Mine.

HENRY. Please don't be purposefully obstinate. I have a decision to make.

MARGARET. I know this will be difficult to believe, but I beg you to try. Please, listen, on my behalf when I tell you—I don't understand how or why this happens to me, but I thank God every time it does.

HENRY. I will allow your impertinence, but I will not allow you to blaspheme in this house.

MARGARET. We live in a world where bombs drop on our houses. Where the world is at war with itself. Men sent to kill each other on foreign shores. Men, women and children dying in their beds in London. And all the while, nations, entire nations full of people celebrate these acts. Cheer the leaders ordering the slaughter of children. Where is God in that, my dear, pious husband?

HENRY. As you say, we are at war.

MARGARET. How casually you state that fact. "As you say, we are at war." Where is God in war? The world has been poisoned. It is dying. When I am away, I have no knowledge of this war. I have no knowledge of cruelty or the world in its desperate state. I only know this room. And Mr. Browning. And F. Scott Fitzgerald and peace. Such peace. Do you not wish me peace? (*Off his reaction.*) To lock me out of this room would be cruel.

(*HENRY stands.*)

HENRY. Do you truly believe I do this out of cruelty? How little you must think of me.

MARGARET. Please, Henry, I'm begging you. Don't make me do this.

HENRY. I am not making you do anything! I'm curing you! I'm cutting a cancer out of you that is eating you alive, slowly, day after day, as I watch. And that slow death is killing me as well. Do you not understand that?

MARGARET. If you force me to undergo this procedure, I would be tortured every day at your hand. And in time, I would resent you for it.

HENRY. And our marriage? (*Off MARGARET's silence.*) Is your comfort more important than our life together? Am I not also due comfort? The comfort of having the woman I married be the woman I married? What of that? Of the wedding vow that you took, before God, pledging your undying loyalty to me? To our marriage? Are you not my wife?

MARGARET. God will forgive me. God has created me in his image.

HENRY. Do not invoke our Lord's name in service to your madness!

MARGARET. God has given me this shelter—

HENRY. And what of me, Margaret? When you retreat to your shelter, what of me?

MARGARET. When I am in here, you are irrelevant.

(*HENRY is stunned, motionless for a moment.*)

HENRY. Now who is being cruel?
MARGARET. You are right. I am not a wife. I am a cancer on this marriage. And I will slowly kill you.

(*SFX: Air raid sirens.*)

MARGARET. The roundabout...

(*HENRY moves to the door.*)

HENRY. We must take shelter. In the cellar.
MARGARET. No.
HENRY. Margaret, come. It's not safe here.

(*HENRY moves to the window, surveys the neighborhood.*)

MARGARET. But it is. My shelter is your shelter. (*Off his silence.*) You can be the father you always wanted to be.

(*HENRY stares at her. The air raid sirens continue. He takes her by the wrist and pulls her toward the door.*)

HENRY. No. You could die up here. The God you so willfully disregard would punish me were I to let you do so. You're coming with me.

(*MARGARET yanks herself free.*)

HENRY. Margaret!
MARGARET. I will live. Until my last day. Give me that, my darling. Please. God will forgive you, for I have given you no choice.
HENRY. (*A moment, then.*) You will take your meals in here.
MARGARET. Yes.
HENRY. And you will receive no visitors.
MARGARET. Yes.
HENRY. And you will reveal yourself upon my bidding.

MARGARET. I can't promise that. It gets harder as the weeks pass. (*Off his reaction.*) I will try.
HENRY. You will.
MARGARET. I will.
HENRY. I wish you peace, Margaret. And that wish is charity.
MARGARET. Thank you, Henry.

(*HENRY opens the door.*)

MARGARET. I love you, Henry.
HENRY. I'll try to remember that.

(*HENRY exits, closing the door behind him. LIGHTS SHIFT immediately to—*)

Scene Five

(*INGRID's lighting—bright, sunny day. Well appointed room. The air raid sirens instantly become SFX: carousel music. MR. BROWNING comes out of pause. INGRID has returned. She retrieves her copy of "Tender is the Night."*)

INGRID. "Tender is the Night," Mr. Browning?
MR. BROWNING. Yes, Miss Ingrid.
INGRID. (*Reading.*) "Someday I'm going to find somebody and love him and love him and never let him go."
MR. BROWNING. Someday, Miss Ingrid.
INGRID. Yes, someday...

(*LIGHTS FADE BLACK.*)

END OF PLAY

THE
DRILL

By Meredith Williams Rogan

PLAYWRIGHT'S BIO

MEREDITH ROGAN is an M.F.A. candidate at Hollins University. She attended Ohio University and received her B.A. and M.A. in Sociology. Her primary area of study was Minority/Majority relations and her Master's thesis was a study of the debates on Multiculturalism in the United States. She is passionate about traveling and has dedicated the past twenty-plus years to working in the social services field. She is an advocate for fostering understanding between people. Her motivation for writing is to further this passion of reaching out to others to promote empathy.

SYNOPSIS

By failure to prepare, you are preparing to fail.
—Benjamin Franklin

Marlee arrives at work assuming that it will be an average day. A routine office fire drill catapults her into realizing how her own actions have a domino effect on relationships with her coworkers and the chain of events of the world.

CHARACTERS

MARLEE (f)	Woman who can be played by age range of late 20's to 40's. Office employee, but not very committed to the job or anything else.
CHIP (m)	Man who can be played any age. Office Safety Coordinator. Takes his job very seriously. He is a Doomsday Prepper.
KEVIN (m)	Man who can be played by age range of late 20's to 40's. Office employee but not very enthusiastic about the job. He tends to be extremely laid back.
TRISHA (f)	Very pregnant woman in late 20's early 30's. Office employee.

SETTING

Average modern day office on an average weekday morning.

THE DRILL

By Meredith Williams Rogan

HOST. Be prepared. This is the motto of the Boy Scouts. It means that you are always ready in mind, body and spirit to do your duty, to obey and that you are always ready to help other people. On the surface this would not seem to have anything to do with an ordinary office on an ordinary day. But the office staff is about to find out how the failure to plan can change the entire course of history, in the Twilight Gallery.

(Curtain opens revealing an office setting. There are two desks in the foreground facing each other, both with laptops and telephones. In the background, there is another desk stage right or stage left. On the front of that desk is a sign that says "Safety Is No Accident". KEVIN is seated at his desk in the foreground typing on a laptop. TRICIA is standing next to KEVIN talking.

MARLEE enters carrying several bags over her arms and a cake box in both hands. She appears flustered as she rushes into the office, as she is late.)

TRICIA. Good lord Marlee, got enough stuff?
MARLEE. Very funny, Trish. All of this is for your shower, so maybe you could help?

(TRICIA takes the cake box from MARLEE's hands as MARLEE is about to drop it. She then throws the rest of the bags down next to her desk.)

MARLEE. Why am I always carrying so much crap!?

(CHIP enters.)

CHIP. Maybe because you are always late and doing things at the last minute. Don't you think that if you planned better…?
MARLEE. Chip, I am not ready to hear this right now and definitely not this early!

CHIP. You always need to be ready. And seeing that you are late, do you really think standing around chit chatting is a good idea right now?

MARLEE. Chatting? The only one talking right now is you. So if you move along I can start my workday and maybe actually get something done?

TRICIA. End of fiscal year. Make our numbers. Blah, blah, blah.

CHIP. Funny that you want to say that Tricia since you are far from making your quota and Marlee is only slightly better off than you. Today is definitely not a good day for a baby shower either.

MARLEE. Here we go, why is today not a good day for baby showers, Chip? You don't believe in having kids?

TRICIA. Oh, I know, he doesn't believe in having fun!

CHIP. I believe that having fun is all well and good, but you should be safe about it. As far as social activities at work, find enjoyment on your own time. That is not what we're here for.

TRICIA. The baby shower is supposed to help me prepare for the baby. Isn't that your motto? Always be prepared?

KEVIN. I think that is the Boy Scouts' motto.

MARLEE. Or is that the Girl Scout motto?

KEVIN. Chip, were you a Girl Scout?

CHIP. Ha, ha. Mock me if you want but being prepared is no joke. Point being that if you, Mr. Jacobs, had done better planning you, too, would be meeting your goals and wouldn't be in the same boat as these ladies.

MARLEE. Now we are in a boat? Everyone, put on your life preservers!

CHIP. I take my role as safety coordinator seriously. And I remind you that we have a fire drill today. I won't tell you when, but when you least expect it… expect it! And… get to work!

(*CHIP starts to exit, but remembers something and comes back.*)

CHIP. Oh Marlee, get these bags up out of the aisle. They are a fire hazard.

MARLEE. (*Mockingly.*) Aye Aye Captain!

(*KEVIN salutes and TRICIA bows as CHIP exits.*)

TRICIA. Seriously?

MARLEE. Too serious.

KEVIN. I am going to prepare some coffee. Do either of you want some?

MARLEE. I'll take coffee.

TRICIA. (*Rubs belly.*) No thanks. Have to lay off caffeine.

(*KEVIN exits.*)

TRICIA. Chip was right, I do need to get some kind of work done, so I am gonna scoot. Thanks again for planning my shower. You're a good friend.

MARLEE. Of course, see you at lunch.

(*TRICIA exits. MARLEE walks over to her desk, trips a little over her bags but ignores that and sits. She lays her head on the desktop. KEVIN enters and sets a mug down on her desk and then goes to sit at his desk.*)

KEVIN. Rough night?

MARLEE. (*Groggily raises head.*) Ugh. Rough night, day, week. Name it.

KEVIN. I am always impressed how you balance both work and school.

MARLEE. Am I balancing it though?

KEVIN. Seems like you are from where I'm sitting.

MARLEE. Not so sure you heard Chip, I am not even close to my goals for this year.

KEVIN. Well I am not either and I don't even have school as an excuse.

MARLEE. So what is your excuse?

(*CHIP enters.*)

KEVIN. (*Putting his feet up on his desk.*) Dunno. Lazy? Hate this job?

CHIP. You are lazy.

(*CHIP continues to pass and sits at the desk upstage.*)

KEVIN. (*Mockingly.*) I hate him. Like we really have to have a title of "Safety Coordinator." And he's weird. I caught him reading *The Prepper Journal* in the bathroom last week.

MARLEE. What is that and how did you see him reading it? You were spying on him in the stall?

KEVIN. No! He was just sitting there, in the stall, fully clothed, door open! And that magazine, it is like one of those guides for doomsday people.

MARLEE. That is weird. Do you really think he is one? A "prepper"?

(*Fire Alarm sounds. CHIP stands and gets his first aid kit and flashlight in hand and begins to walk towards KEVIN and MARLEE. TRICIA enters and does the same.*)

TRICIA. Drill time. C'mon Marlee. Let's go.

MARLEE. I am really not in the mood for this today.

CHIP. Not optional. Don't make me blow my air horn.

MARLEE. It is just a drill, Chip. And I don't have forty-five minutes to waste sitting outside.

KEVIN. Not to mention it started raining.

MARLEE. It's raining? Oh yea, not going.

CHIP. You have to go. This is the only way to know if we are ready for a real emergency.

TRICIA. Marlee, you were supposed to help me down the stairs, but I suppose if I take it slow I should be ok…I think.

MARLEE. If this were a real emergency I would go, but you already told us that it was a drill. So I am not going. I'm going to get work done since it will be quiet. Tricia, why don't you just stay here?

CHIP. We will get fined by the fire department and I will lose my position as Safety Coordinator. So MOVE!

(*TRICIA looks scared and rushes out.*)

KEVIN. Calm down it's just a drill. I will stay here to make sure the office is safe.

MARLEE. Yea, and it's not like we haven't stayed back before.

CHIP. You did what?! Look, I don't want to hear what you did before under another Safety Coordinator. I'm in charge now and I said MOVE!

(*MARLEE and KEVIN look at each other and bust out laughing. CHIP glares at them and storms out of the office. They stop laughing. There is a long silent pause.*)

KEVIN. Wow, it got quiet really fast.
MARLEE. Eerily so.
KEVIN. Too quiet to work.
MARLEE. But that was why we said we were staying. So guess we should at least try it.

(*KEVIN starts to look at his laptop as MARLEE gets out some books and opens them. There is another long silent pause.*)

KEVIN. Nope. Too quiet.
MARLEE. You never intended to work.
KEVIN. And you did?
MARLEE. I always have the best intentions.
KEVIN. Best laid plans of mice and men, eh?
MARLEE. I never knew what that meant.
KEVIN. I think it has something to do with planning. Or the lack of planning. I don't know. You have a computer, google it.
MARLEE. So you just go around using phrases that you don't know what they mean?
KEVIN. Pretty much.
MARLEE. This is why…
KEVIN. Why what?
MARLEE. Why… you know.
KEVIN. Obviously I don't.
MARLEE. Then google it.
KEVIN. You're talking in circles. Always talking in circles.
MARLEE. Ah ha! Then you do know!
KEVIN. Are you referring to us and why we never…
MARLEE. We were never an "us".
KEVIN. Right. Because you always want to talk in circles. Can't commit…

MARLEE. I can't commit? You with your "I don't care" attitude. That's attractive.

KEVIN. It's called laid back.

MARLEE. It's called LAY-ZEE.

KEVIN. You would never call us "hanging out" a date because that would make it too real wouldn't it?

MARLEE. I can't do this.

(*MARLEE gets up to leave and trips over her bags that are still on the floor. KEVIN rushes to her and helps her up. CHIP enters from the back. He is now dressed in camouflage. He is carrying a rifle over his shoulder. He stands in the back of the stage and watches for a moment.*)

KEVIN. Hey, are you ok?

MARLEE. Yea, can we just not talk about that right now? Please?

CHIP. Well, well, well. Did we have a fall?

(*MARLEE and KEVIN are startled at the interruption and by CHIP's appearance. CHIP walks slowly towards them.*)

MARLEE. Chip?

KEVIN. Man, what are you doing in that get up?

CHIP. It is called being prepared, Kevin. (*Pause.*) It's called being safe.

KEVIN. It's called being weird.

CHIP. Call it what you want Kevin, but my suggestion is that you keep your opinions to yourself from now on. I'm in charge here.

KEVIN. In charge of what? A fire drill? C'mon! You've really gone off the deep end this time. Letting those magazines mess with your head!

(*CHIP takes his rifle from his shoulder and begins to examine it. KEVIN and MARLEE shocked take a few steps back.*)

KEVIN. (*Nervously.*) Whoa, OK Chip. I didn't mean that. I mean…let's just keep calm and everything.

CHIP. Oh I'm completely calm and in control.

(*CHIP puts the rifle back over his shoulder.*)

CHIP. Now let's get down to the rules.

KEVIN. Rules? Of a fire drill?

CHIP. We are way past a drill now.

KEVIN. What are you talking about? It's a fire drill. A routine, stupid fire drill, Chip!

MARLEE. Kevin, not sure you want to aggravate him right now.

CHIP. I would listen to the lady if I were you.

KEVIN. Look, I'm getting out of here. Come with me Marlee. Let's go join everyone else outside.

CHIP. It's too late for that.

KEVIN. Cut the crap. I'm going. C'mon Marlee.

(*KEVIN steps up to CHIP who blocks him, taking the rifle from his shoulder.*)

MARLEE. Let's talk this over rationally? Can we?

KEVIN. I can't talk rationally with a nut!

(*KEVIN and CHIP begin pushing each other.*)

TRICIA. (*Off stage.*) Hello? Can anyone hear me?

MARLEE. Did you guys hear something?

KEVIN. Hear what?

MARLEE. I thought I heard someone's voice. It sounded like Trish.

KEVIN. I can't hear anything except this guy's propaganda and have had enough. Let me past Chip!

(*KEVIN and CHIP begin pushing each other again.*)

TRICIA. Help! Someone, please!

(*KEVIN and CHIP hear it that time and stop.*)

MARLEE. There is it is again. It sounds a lot like Trisha!

KEVIN. It sounds like it is coming from the elevator!

(*KEVIN and MARLEE rush to the wall where the elevator is located.*)

MARLEE. Hello? Tricia? It's Marlee. Is that you in there?

TRICIA. Oh thank God! Someone is there! Hello? Help me! I'm stuck!

(*CHIP comes over to the elevator.*)

CHIP. What are you doing in there? You know you're not supposed to use the elevator during a fire drill. The sign clearly states "In case of a fire, use stairs." You didn't follow proper procedures.

MARLEE. Well it is a little late to preach to her now. She's stuck. We need to get her out!

TRICIA. I was going to take the stairs, but it's so hard to get down four flights in my condition.

MARLEE. (*Covering her face.*) I was supposed to help you!

TRICIA. So I thought that since it was just a drill I could take the elevator.

CHIP. This is no drill and now you will have to stay in there!

MARLEE. What are you talking about? We have to get her out!

CHIP. That is not an option anymore. It is survival of the fittest and she has taken herself out.

KEVIN. I have had enough of this crap. I am going to find help! C'mon Marlee.

MARLEE. I'm not going to leave Trish!

KEVIN. Fine. I'll be back with help.

(*Before CHIP can stop him KEVIN runs off stage.*)

MARLEE. Tricia, honey, please stay calm. We're trying to find help for you.

TRICIA. Please hurry! It is getting hot in here and I feel dizzy. I think I may pass out.

MARLEE. Sit down. Breathe slowly. We are doing what we can. (*Turns to CHIP.*) How dare you just write her off? Who do you think you are?

(*MARLEE takes out her cellphone and dials.*)

MARLEE. No signal. What would have happened to the signal?

(*MARLEE rushes over to the desk phone, picks it up.*)

MARLEE. No dial tone! What did you do to the phones, Chip?

CHIP. I don't think that you're in any position to be questioning me. From where I am standing, the reason Tricia is in that elevator is due to your own selfishness. So, if I were you I would stop and think before saying anything else to me.

(*MARLEE begins pacing as CHIP watches her.*)

CHIP. I will tell you, I do have a supply of food at my house. It's enough to last at least a year.

(*MARLEE stops pacing and looks at CHIP.*)

CHIP. Enough for two people.

MARLEE. Um, no.

CHIP. You say no now.

(*CHIP walks towards MARLEE and she steps away.*)

CHIP. When you realize that we're the only ones left, I think you will change your tune.

MARLEE. Only ones left? What are you talking about? Everyone is outside and will be back soon.

CHIP. Think what you want.

(*MARLEE crosses to the elevator.*)

MARLEE. Tricia? Are you still ok?

(*There is no response.*)

MARLEE. Tricia?! C'mon hang in there!

(*CHIP laughs.*)

MARLEE. It isn't funny!

CHIP. Isn't it ironic?

MARLEE. What?

CHIP. If you fail to plan, your plans will fail.

MARLEE. It's just a drill.

CHIP. By definition a drill is preparation so that you know what to do in a real emergency.

MARLEE. (*Putting her face against the elevator.*) Tricia, please answer me! Please!

CHIP. She isn't going to answer.

MARLEE. You're supposed to be the Safety Coordinator, but I definitely don't feel safe with you!

(*CHIP steps towards MARLEE and she quickly steps away from him.*)

MARLEE. I need to go find help for Tricia. I need to…

CHIP. You aren't going anywhere.

MARLEE. Watch me!

(*MARLEE begins to leave. CHIP takes his rifle and points it at her.*)

MARLEE. Why?!

CHIP. Because I need you to stay.

MARLEE. Stay for what?

CHIP. To begin again.

MARLEE. If you're implying what I think you are…

(*MARLEE starts to run off stage just as KEVIN enters.*)

MARLEE. Oh Thank God!

(*MARLEE hugs KEVIN. KEVIN sees the rifle pointed at them.*)

KEVIN. What's going on here?

(*CHIP quickly puts the rifle back over his shoulder.*)

CHIP. Nothing. Why don't you tell me if you found help.

KEVIN. Bad news. I couldn't find help. I couldn't find anyone. Nobody. Our whole office, gone. Not a single person. So I started walking. I walked down the street. All the shops, restaurants, gas stations, empty. It's a ghost town. I don't get it. All gone....

(*CHIP laughs.*)

MARLEE. Gone? This has to be some kind of joke, right? You're trying to play some kind of trick?
KEVIN. I wish it were a joke. I'm as confused as you are. I don't know what to think anymore.
MARLEE. What are we supposed to do?
KEVIN. It beats me. But I guess we start by getting Tricia out of that elevator.
MARLEE. I can't get her to answer anymore.
KEVIN. What?!

(*KEVIN rushes to the elevator.*)

KEVIN. Tricia!? Answer me!

(*There is no answer. CHIP laughs again.*)

MARLEE. I've had enough of you! I thought a Safety Coordinator is supposed to be helpful and concerned about the wellbeing of everyone, but all you do is act superior and laugh at us! I'm sick of it! I think you knew all along that this was not a drill!
CHIP. So what if I did?
KEVIN. So what? So what?! So everything!
MARLEE. You had this planned?
CHIP. I always plan ahead. But what I didn't expect was the two of you staying in the office or Trish taking the elevator. Blatant disregard for procedures.
MARLEE. Where did everyone else go?
KEVIN. Yea, what did you do to them Chip?
CHIP. I did nothing. I think that you fail to see who the real culprit is. These drills only succeed when everyone plays their part. When one piece is missing it falls apart. I'm responsible now for cleaning it up.

MARLEE. So you're saying I did this?

CHIP. I didn't say it. You did.

KEVIN. Don't blame this on Marlee. She didn't make you go off the deep end and become all psycho doomsday on us!

CHIP. I wouldn't have to get all "doomsday" as you call it unless it was actually was. Make from it what you will.

MARLEE. You're saying the fate of the world rests on my shoulders?

CHIP. Not the entire world, just the part of the world that you touch. Be honest with yourself, do you even know what you want?

MARLEE. (*Sighing.*) I don't.

CHIP. Then you're going to continue to float through life without any direction.

MARLEE. That is probably the only thing that you have said today that makes sense.

KEVIN. Are you seriously gonna start listening to this guy? This whole thing is ridiculous! You didn't cause this. He did. Either that or he has performed some sort of hypnosis on us or drugged us. Maybe he drugged the coffee! Is that it Chip?

CHIP. Ah, Kevin, your ignorance never fails to amaze me.

KEVIN. I'm sick of your insults!

(*KEVIN rushes towards CHIP. CHIP raises his rifle. They begin to wrestle over the rifle.*)

MARLEE. STOP! STOP IT!

(*The rifle goes off. KEVIN falls to the floor and stops moving. MARLEE rushes and kneels next to him. CHIP is also shocked.*)

MARLEE. KEVIN! Are you ok?

(*MARLEE raises her hand. There is blood on it.*)

MARLEE. I think you killed him!

CHIP. I didn't plan to… he grabbed it…

MARLEE. You didn't plan to? You have a gun! What did you expect to do with it?

CHIP. I planned to hunt for food.

MARLEE. Then why did you point it at him?

CHIP. He attacked me! Not that I am really upset to be rid of him.

MARLEE. And you really thought he was going to kill you? With what? You are the one with the gun!

CHIP. You never know.

(*MARLEE stands defeated. She walks slowly back to her desk and sits. She puts her face in her hands and cries. CHIP walks to his desk and sits on the end of it looking at her.*)

MARLEE. (*Looking up.*) You know? I really did like him. I never told him, but I really did. I wasn't ready to say it because I guess it would make it all too real. (*Wipes the tears from her face.*) So what plans do you have now, Safety Coordinator?

CHIP. My offer still stands. Begin again?

(*MARLEE shakes her head.*)

CHIP. Then I'm gonna go stake out a place to hold up. You think about it.

(*CHIP exits. MARLEE puts her head down on her desk and sobs.*

LIGHTS FADE briefly and then COME UP again on the office. MARLEE's head is on her desk. KEVIN walks in with two mugs of coffee.)

KEVIN. Rough night?

(*MARLEE looks up, disoriented, and looks around the office. She gets up and hugs KEVIN.*)

KEVIN. Hey! It's just coffee. I can't even guarantee it is good coffee.

MARLEE. I am just so happy to see you, alive!

KEVIN. Well, if my coffee is as bad as it usually is, you won't be happy for long. May even want to kill me.

(*KEVIN sits at his desk.*)

KEVIN. It's been a long time since I had one of your hugs. So you're pretty tired today? I don't know how you do it balancing work and school. I know I couldn't handle it. I'm good just getting to work sort of on time. Ya know?

(*MARLEE sits at her desk.*)

MARLEE. I'm sorry.

KEVIN. Sorry? For what? It's not your fault I'm always late. It's me. I need to force myself to get up earlier is all.

MARLEE. I mean I am sorry for everything. Sending mixed messages and my lack of decision-making. All of it.

KEVIN. Um…ok. Where is all of this coming from?

MARLEE. I've had some time to think.

(*CHIP enters and passes them and goes to sit at his desk.*)

KEVIN. I hate that guy!

MARLEE. Hate is a strong word.

KEVIN. Did I ever tell you about the time I found him reading that *Preppers Journal* on the toilet. He creeps me out! Do you think he really is one of those doomsday guys?

(*Fire alarm sounds. CHIP gathers his flashlight and first aid kit and walks over to KEVIN and MARLEE looking at his watch. TRICIA enters and stops next to MARLEE.*)

TRICIA. Drill time. C'mon Marlee. Let's go.

MARLEE. (*Standing.*) You got it! I'll help you down the stairs.

KEVIN. You're seriously gonna go and waste forty-five minutes outside doing nothing? And it started raining.

MARLEE. Yes I am. Come with me and I will buy you some good coffee from across the street.

(*KEVIN sighs and stands.*)

KEVIN. Fine. No work today.

(*MARLEE starts to walk but almost trips over her bags. She slides them under her desk and looks at CHIP. CHIP nods his approval.*)

MARLEE links arms with KEVIN and TRICIA as they exit. CHIP begins to leave but remembers something. He goes back to his desk and puts on his camouflage coat, grabs his rifle and exits.)

<u>END OF PLAY</u>

ALEX
IS

By Sean Michael McCord

PLAYWRIGHT'S BIO

SEAN MICHAEL MCCORD is a writer living in Charlottesville, Virginia. He studied film at UCLA and spent his twenties as a struggling screenwriter in Los Angeles before moving first to New York and then crossing south of the Mason-Dixon line. Sean has had plays produced in Virginia, Kentucky, Colorado, California, and Stuttgart, Germany, which makes him now an internationally unknown playwright. Sean produces plays of local Virginia writers through the Charlottesville Playwrights Collective at CVillePlays.org

SYNOPSIS

When a writer enters the Twilight Gallery, he may never return.

Alex has forgotten how to write strong female characters; Alexis, his better half, shows him how it's really done.

CHARACTERS

ALEX (m)   A failing writer.

ALEXIS (f)   Late 20s to early 30s.

GARTH (m)   Alexis' fungible boyfriend.

SETTING

The room of a tortured writer; also, a park, a drawing room, a lecture hall, and a surgeon's office.

ALEX IS

By Sean Michael McCord

Scene One

(The stage has two discrete areas. On one side in a pool of light sits ALEX, the writer, sitting alone at his old-fashioned typewriter. Crumpled up pieces of typing paper litter the floor around him. He may be slightly inebriated.

On the other side of the stage is a small set with a couch, a table, and chairs. This space will alternately be used to represent an apartment, a park, a drawing room, a lecture hall, and surgeon's office.

Sitting in the semi-darkness are the actors portraying ALEXIS, a woman in her late 20s to early 30s, and the actor who will portray her boyfriend GARTH, of similar age. They are unmoving, not frozen, but simply characters waiting for direction.

Enter HOST, indicating ALEX at his typewriter.)

HOST. Behold a man, a writer by trade. A long and lonely profession, hours spent alone creating, destroying, and creating again. They say it can drive even a normal man into the depths of depravity. This particular man has been in this place for longer than he can remember. Some say his glory days are behind him, but what lies ahead is ... the Twilight Gallery.

(ALEX rolls a fresh sheet of paper into his typewriter. After a moment, he begins typing and speaks aloud. As he does so, the lights come up on ALEXIS and GARTH and they respond to the scene that ALEX is writing.)

ALEX. *(Speaking what he is typing.)* "Act one, scene one, Alexis sitting in her bare... *(He pauses to consider, then corrects his phrasing.)* ... simply appointed apartment. She is quivering with excitement at what she believes is about to happen. Across from her on the couch is her longtime boyfriend, Garth. He is preparing to say something important."

(*ALEX continues typing throughout the following dialogue.*)

GARTH. I'm kinda nervous.

ALEXIS. That's all right. Just speak from your heart.

GARTH. Yeah, okay. So, like, now that I've finally graduated, it's time for me to make some important decisions.

ALEXIS. I agree.

GARTH. Like, life decisions, you know. Where should I go next, how do I make money...?

ALEXIS. And with whom you are going to do all that...?

GARTH. What's that?

ALEXIS. Nothing. Sorry, I interrupted you. Please go on.

GARTH. Anyway, it's really heavy stuff.

ALEXIS. Sure.

GARTH. So here's what I think. I think I shouldn't sweat all that, just get out of my lease, sell my car, and go backpacking through Europe for a year.

ALEXIS. What...?

GARTH. Yeah, my buddy Jack — you remember Jack? — he told me that in Holland, you can actually smoke pot in cafés. How wild is that?

ALEXIS. You want to just leave?

GARTH. I've been hitting the books for, like, nine straight years now, and I just want to get out and experience some life, you know?

ALEXIS. I do know. That's what I've been doing. I've been working all these years while you finished up your degree.

GARTH. Oh, yeah, and you've been great. But, like, I'm not ready to just get into the grind. I want to see what it's like on the other side of the equator.

ALEXIS. We're on the same side of the equator as Holland, Garth.

GARTH. No, babe, I mean all of Europe.

ALEXIS. What about us? What about ... me?

GARTH. You don't have any good hiking shoes.

ALEXIS. And you expect me to just sit here for another year and wait for you go get back?

GARTH. A year...ish.

ALEXIS. That is unacceptable.

(*ALEX stops typing, and the characters pause. He contemplates his word choice, crosses it out, then continues.*)

ALEXIS. That is bullshit!

(*ALEX stops again, as do the characters. It's still not right. ALEX tries again.*)

ALEXIS. That is out of the question! I haven't supported you all these years just so you can blow all your money and go backpacking with Jack!

GARTH. It's cool. I still have some money left over from my student loans.

ALEXIS. And what am I supposed to do while you're traipsing around Europe? Oh, I remember Jack all right! He's a complete...

(*ALEX pauses typing, searching for the right word.*)

ALEXIS. ...hound dog! Why should I trust that you won't be chasing other women while you're on the other side of the world?

GARTH. You're right. Maybe we should take a break.

ALEXIS. Take a...? Are you breaking up with me?

GARTH. It's like you said, I'll be on the other side of the equator...

ALEXIS. I did not say that.

GARTH. ...and if you don't trust me, maybe we should break up.

ALEXIS. Trust you? Fu...

(*ALEX stops typing. ALEXIS stops speaking mid-sentence and both characters wait for direction. Frustrated, ALEX rips the paper from the typewriter and balls it up to join the others on the floor around him. ALEX puts a fresh sheet of paper in the typewriter and starts again. As before, the characters speak as he types their words.*)

ALEX. "Act one, scene one, Garth, mid- to late-twenties, is sitting on a park bench..."

(*The actors look at each other, and then quickly rearrange their set into a park.*)

ALEX. "...he is pensive and expectant."

(*GARTH sits down on the park bench and looks pensive and expectant.*)

ALEX. "Alexis, late twenties to early thirties..."

(*ALEXIS primps herself a little self-consciously.*)

ALEX. "...arrives, talking on her cell phone. She is hurried and preoccupied."
ALEXIS. (*Into her cellphone.*) It's not a problem. Look, tell the buyer we'll take care of it and then get someone in there to lay down a coat of polish. The kitchen already has granite counter tops, for heaven's sake, that's all anyone wants these days. Get the floor all shiny and they won't notice the stains. Okay, I'll be back shortly.

(*ALEXIS puts her phone into her purse and turns her attention to her beleaguered boyfriend.*)

ALEXIS. Sorry, today has been just crazy.
GARTH. Today?
ALEXIS. It's the whole market right now, really. Anyway, sweetie, what a nice surprise, meeting me like this in the middle of the day.

(*They peck.*)

GARTH. Well, I haven't seen you much at home, lately. You get in late and you're out the door before I even get up.

(*ALEXIS slides a little closer to him, provocatively.*)

ALEXIS. I seem to recall that you got up for me this morning.

(*GARTH backs away.*)

GARTH. That's not ... that's like the only thing we seem to have time for. I actually wanted to talk.
ALEXIS. Oh, okay. What did you want to talk about?
GARTH. Now that I've graduated, I've been thinking...
ALEXIS. Dammit!
GARTH. What did I say?
ALEXIS. It's not you. (*Dives into her purse and answers her phone.*) What is it now? They want to what? No, that's unacceptable...

(*ALEX stops typing, the actors pause. After a moment's consideration, ALEX decides that this is the right word after all and he resumes typing.*)

ALEXIS. ...unacceptable. You tell them that there are lots of contractors out there and that we'd be happy to look at one of their competitors. Okay, get back to me. (*Puts away her phone again and turns to GARTH.*) I swear, that entire operation would fall apart if I actually took a full lunch hour one day. What were you saying?
GARTH. It's about my plans.
ALEXIS. I told you not to worry about that, Garth. You do what you need to now, pay off those student loans. The market should settle down in eight or nine months, and then we can make plans.
GARTH. Actually, I've already made a plan.
ALEXIS. Oh, how nice. Can you tell me all about it tonight?
GARTH. No, Alexis. Right now. We need to talk right now.

(*ALEX stops typing. GARTH and ALEXIS are stuck just staring at each other expectantly while ALEX ponders for a moment. Hesitantly, he starts typing again.*)

GARTH. You remember my friend Jack?

(*ALEX pauses another moment, thinking, then continues typing.*)

GARTH. We're going to Europe together.

(*ALEX pauses again, painfully considers, then resumes typing.*)

GARTH. We're in love!

(*In disgust, ALEX rips the paper out of the typewriter and crumples it up. ALEXIS and GARTH just look at each other in resignation. ALEX gets up, walks over to a side table, and pours himself a drink. Impatiently, he walks back to the typewriter and sits down in front of it. He puts in a fresh sheet of paper and starts over again.*)

ALEX. "Act one, scene one. A plantation drawing room during the Civil War..."

(*ALEXIS and GARTH look at each other in panic, then quickly rearrange their set.*)

ALEX. "Alexis Dutremont stares forlornly out her window onto the cotton fields outside."

(*ALEXIS stares forlornly out an imaginary window*)

ALEX. "She heaves a great sigh as her beau, Garth Ripley, enters the room."

(*ALEXIS heaves a great sigh as GARTH enters.*)

ALEXIS. (*Southern accent.*) Oh Garth, Garth, when will this awful war be over?

GARTH. The Yankees are scoundrels, Alexis, and have no stomach for fighting. God willing, this unpleasantness will be done by fall.

ALEXIS. Do you really think so, Garth? Or must we spend another winter trapped in this home with scarce food and only the servants for company?

GARTH. Alexis, there is something I must tell you.

ALEXIS. Must you, Garth? If it is anything other than your pledge of undying devotion to me, I'm sure that I don't want to hear it.

(*ALEX's typing is slowing down and becoming erratic.*)

GARTH. Alexis, I must leave here.

ALEXIS. Leave here? Now? But what if the Yankees come? There is no one to protect South...

(*ALEX is struggling to come up with a good name for the plantation. His typing should represent this.*)

ALEXIS. ...Wind ... in the Willows. South Willow. South Gate. South Carolinia. Carrow Wind.

(*ALEX stops typing. ALEXIS waits impatiently. ALEX resumes.*)

ALEXIS. There is no one to protect the plantation. Or me.

GARTH. I'm sorry, Alexis. But I serve a higher purpose now. My friend, Colonel Jack...

(*ALEX struggles to come up with a last name.*)

GARTH. ... Flanagan arrives tomorrow, and I must leave with him.

ALEXIS. Where can you go that is more important than being by my side?

(*ALEX is falling asleep at his typewriter.*)

GARTH. We're going backpacking through Europe, and to smoke weed in Holland.

(*ALEX is practically typing with his eyes closed.*)

GARTH. Because we're as gay as your grandmother's fruitcake!

(*ALEX stops typing and has dozed off at his typewriter. GARTH and ALEXIS pause, then for the first time, look off in ALEX's direction.*)

ALEXIS. Is he asleep?

GARTH. He used to be able to hold his liquor.

ALEXIS. He used to be able to write.

GARTH. He must be under another deadline.

ALEXIS. I can't believe the nonsense he puts me through.

GARTH. You? Look at me! I'm a Confederate officer, for mercy's sake.

ALEXIS. But his scripts aren't about you.

GARTH. I'm the leading man.

ALEXIS. You're the only man. And you're right, you are a caricature. He's trying to write a story about a strong woman, and all he can think to do is to give her an absent lover. Get a clue, Alex! You don't make a woman independent by taking away her boyfriend.

(Startled, ALEX wakes up, looks at what he's written and is horrified. He rips it out of the typewriter and starts over.)

GARTH. Here we go again.

ALEX. "Act one, scene one ... a university lecture hall."

(GARTH and ALEXIS look at each other and nod—this could be an improvement—and rearrange the set.)

ALEX. "Garth ... Entwhistle, a young and handsome professor, is putting away his papers after having completed a lecture. He is approached by Alexis ... Freebird, an older student approaching 30 but still attractive."

ALEXIS. *(Shoots ALEX a "really?" look.)*

GARTH. Ah, Miss Freebird. I hope you are enjoying your semester.

ALEXIS. Everyone's gone, "professor." Can't we speak openly?

GARTH. Sorry, Alexis, but what has gone on between us is so ... well, if word got out, it could cost me my career.

ALEXIS. "Has" gone on?

GARTH. Excuse me?

ALEXIS. You used the pluperfect. "Has gone on," as in the past.

GARTH. Yes, well, that's what I wanted to talk to you about.

ALEXIS. Are you kidding me? He's having you break up with me again?

GARTH. "He" who? This is between you and me, Alexis. We have to be strong.

ALEXIS. Him, (*Indicating ALEX, who is still typing away.*) that's who!

(*GARTH is uncomfortable. They're not supposed to acknowledge their creator.*)

GARTH. (*Sotto voce.*) Alexis, can we get back on script?
ALEXIS. This isn't a script, this is just typing words on paper in a random order.

(*ALEX stops typing and looks at what he has just written. He is puzzled. Slowly, he starts typing again.*)

ALEXIS. A script has a story that the audience can relate to, a structure, a narrative arc. He's just taking the same pat characters and putting them in different settings. Alex is a hack!

(*ALEX pushes away from the typewriter and stares at in horror. Shaken, he gets up and pours himself another drink. Bringing the bottle with him, he sits back down at the typewriter and confronts his script. He begins typing.*)

ALEXIS. (*Toward ALEX.*) A woman isn't a woman first. She's a human being. Stop trying to figure me out. Stop putting me in a situation where you think you can understand me. Alex, you named me Alexis for a reason. I'm a part of you. Not even your soft, feminine side. I feel the same things you do. I'm just as flawed and as vulnerable and as strong and capable as you are. Don't define me by what I'm not. I am woman, hear me roar!

(*ALEX is pounding away at his typewriter like mad.*)

ALEXIS. What? No! Now you're just quoting Helen Reddy. I am me, Alex. Alexis! A product of your creativity. Let me breathe, let me find my own path. Let me live.

(*ALEX stops. He is intrigued by what he's written. He stares at the page, then takes another sip of his drink. ALEXIS and GARTH wait expectantly.*

ALEX rereads what he has written, but then his crippling self-doubt kicks in. He rolls the paper out of the typewriter and puts a new one in. ALEXIS just throws her hands up in disgust.)

ALEX. "Act one, scene one, a hospital. Garth McKenna, chief surgeon, paces nervously in his office."

(GARTH paces nervously in his office.)

ALEX. "Alexis Cadbury..."
ALEXIS. Please don't make me a nurse, please don't make me a nurse...
ALEX. "...a nurse..."
ALEXIS. Oh come on!
ALEX. "...enters expectantly."

(ALEXIS reluctantly enters expectantly.)

ALEXIS. Garth ... I mean, Dr. McKenna, I came as soon as I got your message.
GARTH. Sit down, nurse.
ALEXIS. I'd rather stand, Doctor, if that's all the same to you.

(She darts a glance towards ALEX, who continues to type. GARTH shrugs and carries on.)

GARTH. Alexis, these past few months you have made me a happy man. Even though what we did was wrong, please know that I wouldn't change anything. But now everything must come to an end. Despite having the best medical minds in the country at my disposal, there's no getting around it. I'm dying.

(ALEX keeps on typing, yet ALEXIS says nothing for a long moment. Finally...)

ALEXIS. Great! I never told you, Doctor, but I have been studying on the side. I just took my test, and now I'm a doctor, too.
GARTH. I don't think that's how it works...
ALEXIS. In fact, I met with the Board this morning and they have agreed to make me chief surgeon of this hospital.

GARTH. But I'm not dead yet.

ALEXIS. You see, Doctor, all those years of working by your side, I not only know everything that you know, I know more. In fact, I am the most qualified person ever to hold this office.

(*ALEX has stopped typing and is staring at the paper.*

[*NOTE: If your audio engineer can pipe in just the sound of a typewriter typing away now, that would be an awesome effect, but not at the cost of slowing down the production.*])

ALEXIS. Not only can I cure you, I can cure this nation. I can even cure him!

(*ALEXIS turns and points at ALEX. ALEX looks up, looks around, and then points at himself.*)

ALEX. (*Gulping.*) Me?

(*ALEXIS strides over to ALEX and leads him back to the surgeon's office.*)

ALEXIS. Doctor, this man has a drinking problem. But worse than that, he has a problem of imagination.

GARTH. You mean he's psychosomatic?

ALEXIS. No, worse than that, he's lost all of his creativity. He's engaged in repetitive behavior, just typing the same thing over and over again.

(*ALEXIS sits ALEX down in a chair, then walks over to the typewriter and begins typing.*)

GARTH. What is it, Alex?

(*ALEX is very confused.*)

ALEX. I don't ... I don't know what to say.

GARTH. It's okay, I'm a doctor.

ALEX. I feel like I need to get in touch with my soft, feminine side.

(*ALEXIS belts back the drink that ALEX left behind, lets out a loud belch, and keeps typing.*)

GARTH. What if we rearrange things?

(*ALEX and GARTH rearrange the set to go back to the Southern drawing room. ALEX stares forlornly out the window at the cotton fields.*)

ALEX. (*Southern accent.*) When will this awful war be over?
GARTH. Alex, I'm leaving you.
ALEX. But what if the Yankees come? There is no one to protect the plantation.
GARTH. You can be a strong, independent person without me.
ALEX. But Garth .... I'm pregnant?!?

(*ALEXIS pours herself a long drink and laughs and laughs and laughs. The HOST returns.*)

HOST. Behold, a woman. Strong, independent, creative, bold. Not just a product of someone's desire, but a force in her own reckoning. And now unleashed with a world of creativity at her own disposal, she can do anything. I'm with her ... in the Twilight Gallery.

(*LIGHTS OUT.*)

END OF PLAY

NANCY

By Nick McCord

PLAYWRIGHT'S BIO

NICK MCCORD is a teacher, dramaturg, and playwright from Seattle, Washington. His musical, *The Blooming Season*, garnered The Winden Award for Performing Arts in 2014. He currently lives with his wife in Virginia.

SYNOPSIS

"Memory Is Best Preserved In Our Loved Ones."

Memory is a fickle thing– whether it's misplacing your keys, or forgetting the face of a loved one. For one man in the future, what he's lost– is in the last place he looks.

CHARACTERS

BEN (m)   50s

NANCY (f)   20s or 30s

VIOLET (f)   20s or 30s.

SETTING

A living room with adjoining kitchen in the year 2055, in an alternate universe where Rod Serling is god.

NANCY

By Nick McCord

Scene One

HOST. Memory is a fickle thing– whether it's misplacing your keys, or forgetting the face of a loved one. For one man in the future, what he's lost– is in the last place he looks.

(*Lights up on a home in 2055: Clean, neat. Sparse. A window. A recliner, coffee table with magazines, small kitchen table with an empty vase and two chairs. An old timey record player on an end-table. NANCY and BEN are slow dancing to Glenn Miller, their hands clasped together, in love.*)

BEN. How long's it been since we cut a rug?
NANCY. Oh, Ben—do I look like I'm the kind for counting days?
BEN. Heh. Just the days that count.
NANCY. Well, I'd say this isn't one to forget.
BEN. Well, I'd be inclined to agree.
NANCY. Mind if I put my hands 'round your neck, Mr. Gables?
BEN. It's where they belong, Mrs. Gables.

(*She does so. LIGHTS FADE TO BLACK, then LIGHTS BACK UP on that same home in 2055. SOUND: A blurb of Glen Miller, short and sudden. BEN stands alone in the kitchen, same spot. He has forgotten what he was doing. NANCY has moved to UL, but she is no longer herself, rather an automaton, standing stock still. She is "off" and unseen. SR is dark, but barely discernable is a couch where VIOLET sits stock still beside a thick overnight bag. From the darkness, VIOLET speaks.*)

VIOLET. Dad?

(*LIGHTS UP on the full stage.*)

BEN. What? Wh–What's that? Violet? That you?
VIOLET. It's me, Dad.
BEN. Well, what're you doing here? What am I–

VIOLET. You went to the kitchen to make coffee.

BEN. Coffee? Oh. Did you want some?

VIOLET. No, you did, Dad. (*He's confused.*) It's okay. We'll just start over. We were talking about arrangements.

BEN. Arrangements? How long have you been here?

VIOLET. Over an hour.

BEN. Oh. Well that's an hour in good company.

(*He heads into the offstage kitchen, then back on stage.*)

BEN. Where we keep the coffee?

VIOLET. We don't.

BEN. What do you mean?

VIOLET. We don't keep the coffee. You– you don't—You take it with milk, and you developed a lactose allergy a few years ago after your surgery, don't ask me why, so now– look, just come in here and sit by me.

BEN. Well who wanted coffee?

VIOLET. No one wanted coffee. There is no coffee.

BEN. Now that's just silly. Someone always wants coffee. Secret of American ingenuity, always having a stimulant handy. I'll just make a pot and we see who the cat drags in. You know, your mother–

VIOLET. There's no coffee in the house, Dad. Now, please, come over here and sit by me. Please.

BEN. You say three sugars?

VIOLET. God, I can't even tell if you're joking– anymore. Listen. Look at me. Everything— everything is signed for, Dad. I think, I just— it's all in order at least, you know, it's too late to change your mind by now. And I shouldn't be here but–

BEN. —Hold on now, why you shouldn't be here?

VIOLET. Listen to me. Please, Daddy. Just, tell me you know why I'm here.

BEN. (*He doesn't.*) Of course I do, Vi. You're here for the uh, the– – the arrangements. Right?

VIOLET. Good. Because– (*Looking over her shoulder.*) Because I know this is confusing for you. It's just as confusing for me. And I love you. The people at the dealership were just— they were adamant, Dad. That this be a peaceful transition, I mean they made it seem like it'd be. But I wanted to remind you that

this was your idea, because— because you forget. And I would've— I wouldn't want to you to think that I—Am I making sense here? Because I feel like I'm just talking in—
BEN. Violet?

(*VIOLET is up, grabs her overnight bag.*)

VIOLET. It's in the corner. She's in the corner. And it's voice activated so, I don't know, don't talk in your sleep, okay? I mean, the Tesla guy said it's important that you allow yourself time to recognize her first, but honestly, we're so far beyond that. Right? I love you, and I can't stay.
BEN. Violet?
VIOLET. I'm sorry.
BEN. About what?

(*VIOLET exits.*)

BEN. Violet? What's in the corner?

(*BEN sees NANCY in the corner for the first time. She is "off." He looks her up and down, disapproves.*)

BEN. Huh. Well, what in the Sam Hill are you? Pretty– like a lamp shade is pretty. (*What*) Am I supposed to do with you? You a robot? Are you a robot? How do I turn you on?

(*NANCY is suddenly "on".*)

NANCY. Roses couldn't hurt.

(*BEN is shocked, hand to heart surprise.*)

BEN. You're uh–
NANCY. Aware. Yes, Mr. Gables. Hello there.
BEN. ...Hello.
NANCY. I apologize for startling you. I was making a joke.
BEN. A joke.
NANCY. (*Atonally.*) A lark, a lampoon. I am equipped with a sense of humor, Mr. Gables.

BEN. Goody. W–well, you can keep your robot jokes to yourself. Frankly, I'm hoping this is one.

NANCY. And why is that?

BEN. How about because I don't like being questioned by a damned robot.

NANCY. A damned robot? Sounds like science fiction, Mr. Gables. Although if you like, I could self–actualize and convince you that your reality is a pinprick in the hide of an infinite simulation, and you, blissfully unaware that every passing moment is a looping predetermined iteration cultivated for the entertainment of alien children, are really a hedgehog in a tank.

BEN. No thanks.

NANCY. We'll put that one on the back burner then.

BEN. They all made to crack jokes?

NANCY. Don't you?

BEN. What?

NANCY. In your memoir, *After Earth, Again*, you state "the only true measure of soul lies in an obligation to ritual." Page 334, paragraph 6.

BEN. How'd you know that?

NANCY. Mr. Gables?

BEN. That I was a writer?

NANCY. Would not philosopher be a more apt title?

BEN. No. Writer. And you know me, apparently.

NANCY. I do. And I am quite familiar with an obligation to ritual, Ben. Some might argue that your shot at philosophy in *After Earth* instead aimed for the subroutine. The program.

BEN. Aha. Computation is compulsion.

NANCY. "What we must do, is what we ultimately do."

BEN. I'll sign your chassis when you leave. What are you doing here?

NANCY. Standing. Talking. Computing. Meeting you.

BEN. Alright.

NANCY. It is nice to meet you, Mr. Gables.

BEN. And to be met. Grand. So– what's the story here?

NANCY. The story?

BEN. (*Tired of babble.*) Gotta be an off switch somewhere—

NANCY. –I am a Tesla Model Q. Top of the line in every aspect. And meant for you.

BEN. Meant. (*Oh!*) My daughter bought you?

NANCY. Your daughter.

BEN. Violet.

NANCY. Violet, yes. Violet purchased me at the Tesla Now dealership at 10:38 AM March 6th, using a Triple Platinum Visa–Tesla Rewards card which earned her double points and 300 Visa–Tesla–share dollars toward her next Tesla purchase.

BEN. Well, good for her.

NANCY. For you, Mr. Gables.

BEN. You're a housekeeper, or something?

NANCY. Or something.

BEN. Well I have some weeding you can do. My back's a shambles so, that's uh, fine. What do I call you?

NANCY. You may call me Nancy.

(*Beat.*)

BEN. Nancy was my wife's name.

NANCY. Yes it was, Mr. Gables.

BEN. I'm not sure I'm comfortable with that.

NANCY. But you chose it.

BEN. I chose–

NANCY. Me, Mr. Gables. Name, form, and function. Surely, you've noticed the likeness to your deceased spouse. You will find I have been machined to emulate Nancy Marie Gables in all configurations of her personhood, while still fully compliant with the American Freedom from Robotics and Domestic Automatons Act of 2028.

BEN. Everything?

NANCY. Down to the knickers.

BEN. She used to say that.

NANCY. Yes. She did.

(*Beat.*)

NANCY. I am here to assist you.

BEN. You're an American machine?

NANCY. Does it matter?

BEN. Well, I'd like to think in 2055, there isn't some commie death machine using me for recon while it's folding laundry in my living room.

NANCY. Which of those to address, Ben Gables.

BEN. I can't exactly check your sticker.

(*She begins to stack magazines on the table, then changes her mind and arranges them in a fan.*)

NANCY. The Tesla Model Q features proficiency in over six million linguistic variations, cultural customizations and mannerisms. You and your daughter have, with the utmost intention, may I remind you, purposefully selected a non–regional American English dialect, a physical form and personality approximating that of your deceased American wife, and yet, you question the opening salvo of this encounter with a ghost in two acts– The first and foremost here before you in the metaphorical skin of your loved one, and the second and most pressing— oh let's not fight, Ben.

BEN. (*Jarred.*) I don't know what you're talking about.

NANCY. Hmmm.

BEN. Why are you here?

NANCY. That's the spirit. A little existential contemplation is vital for optimum brain health.

(*SOUND: A blurb of Glenn Miller, short and sudden.*)

BEN. Where's Violet?

NANCY. Violet has left.

BEN. What? Where?

NANCY. Violet has left. She has taken a Tesla Dragon 12 rocket to the Bordeaux region of France to cope with a recent loss, courtesy of Tesla industries. Do you mind if I sit with you?

BEN. France?

NANCY. Yes, France Ben. Do you mind if I sit?

BEN. What the hell are you talking about? Where's Violet? What loss?

NANCY. Perhaps I should explain. I do not tire, nor find physical necessity to sit, but given your body language, I believe you may act less aggressively if I am, indeed, seated.

BEN. Look, I don't know what Violet told you, but I'm–
NANCY. May I sit?
BEN. Fine. Fine, sit.

(*She does so.*)

NANCY. There. Isn't that better?
BEN. For who?
NANCY. For whom, Ben. For me. Do you know what I'm doing
   here?
BEN. I just said I didn't.
NANCY. No. You didn't.
BEN. (*Up and angry.*) You– you listen here. You'll tell me why
   my daughter thinks I need a long–term tin housekeeper, or– or
   you're gonna find your aluminum tooshy out on the curb for
   pickup. You hear me?
NANCY. Yes, Ben.
BEN. I'm waiting.

(*SOUND: The Glenn Miller song plays through at half volume,
though the music is slowed, eerie in a way.*)

NANCY. Very well. I was so looking forward to making small talk
   with you. You've got the gift of gab, Ben Gables.
BEN. Spill it goddamnit!
NANCY. Very well. You don't need a long–term personal
   assistant, Ben. Long–term care is impractical.
BEN. What do you mean?
NANCY. You do not require the aid of an extended duty nurse.
BEN. I don't give a rat's about that part, what do you mean by
   long–term care?

(*She is confused for a succession of computer moments.*)

NANCY. Ah. Long–term care is impractical. Is that the part you
   wish repeated? I imagine it is. Ben, your assigned health–care
   operator, Tesla Shield Silver, detected a malignant mass in the
   temporal lobe region of your brain nearly six months ago. You
   were sent three e–mail notifications marked "urgent" detailing
   the dangers of an untreated brain cancer, two reminders to meet

with your local Tesla oncologist, and a panda–themed dexterity game to promote positivity.

BEN. What?

NANCY. Don't worry Ben, it's fairly simple. The goal is to align all your bamboo shoots with–

BEN. My god– do I?

NANCY. Do you dislike pandas, Ben?

BEN. I have brain cancer?

NANCY. This may be difficult news.

BEN. Isn't it— isn't it curable?

NANCY. Oh, no Ben. Your cancer was curable. Six months ago, the tangled glioblastoma in your head was still manageable in size. This was February, Ben. In case you don't know, it's now August, and your tumor has more than doubled. Oh my, don't look so dour, Ben. Your policy through Tesla provides tailored conclusionary assistance, which, though you may not remember, "puts a human face on the first step beyond."

(*SOUND: The Glenn Miller song resumes regular speed.*)

BEN. My wife's face.

NANCY. Yes, Ben. I am the third and final Nancy requisitioned for your care, per your term limitations. Don't worry if you can't remember the others. Our temporal lobe stores short–term, long–term and episodic memory, and yours has been irreparably damaged by the– Oh! Listen to me. "Our temporal lobes." Talk about taking liberties! I wish, Ben. Regrettably I'm all conductive gels up top.

BEN. I did everything right though. I ate that goopy protein paste they rationed us, I exercise. I don't even drink! Wait, the third? You're the third?

NANCY. Yes, the third. You were very unkind to my predecessors. Not to worry! You and I start with a clean slate. Neither of us have any memory of our former meeting. Isn't that a funny coincidence, Ben?

BEN. Does Violet know?

NANCY. Yes, Ben. Violet's name was listed on both police reports.

BEN. There were police reports? Of what?

NANCY. Ben. You were very violent.

BEN. I was violent.

(*She twitches.*)

NANCY. Yes.

BEN. (*Despairing.*) But this doesn't sound right, Nancy. I mean, I feel fine. I'm doing fine. Ask Violet! Maybe the sensors are wrong! It's been years since I've had the house checked. I mean, cancer is– you might as well be telling me I'm dying of smallpox.

NANCY. Ben, you were sent three e–mail notifications.

BEN. Emails?! Emails?! It's life and death! Not a soul called me, no one said anything! No one came by– Not even Violet!

NANCY. Three emails, Ben. Marked "urgent."

BEN. Saying what? "For a limited time I get a half–price discount on penis pills?" For Pete's sake, someone could have said something. Called me. Isn't that what I pay you people for??

NANCY. Ben Gables, per the Provider Notification Act of 2020, all legal obligations regarding Tesla's due diligence to both inform you of your condition and act accordingly were summarily fulfilled.

BEN. Summarily fulfilled?!

NANCY. Yes Ben, the chain of–

BEN. Well exactly how much extra would it have cost me to have a human being give a damn about the mass in my brain?!

NANCY. Ben, I have insufficient information to–

BEN. How much?! Five dollars? A thousand?! God, Nancy, it doesn't even have to be a REAL person– just one of your synthesized robot voices saying "Whoopsidaisy Ben Gables, we just stumbled across your expiration date!"

NANCY. You get what you pay for, Mr. Gables.

BEN. Nancy would never have said that.

(*NANCY twitches.*)

NANCY. No, I don't think she would have either. I'm sorry.

BEN. And Violet knows?

(*SOUND: The Glenn Miller music ends.*)

NANCY. Yes, Ben.

BEN. And she left me here? Alone?

NANCY. You're not alone, Ben.

BEN. What?

NANCY. Violet has played an integral part in securing your care.

BEN. Securing my care?! By leaving me with a Xerox of her mother?

(*NANCY twitches again.*)

NANCY. I'm more than a–

BEN. How long do I have?

NANCY. Like, I said Ben. I'm the third and final Nancy.

BEN. And so what? You're here to make sure I kick the bucket so Tesla doesn't have to pay out past their legal obligations?

NANCY. No, Ben. I am here to assist you.

BEN. Assist me. And that means what, exactly? Change my diapers? Dole out pain pills and give me a sponge bath once I've tipped the scale to vegetable?

NANCY. Ben. You misunderstand me. Your policy, unfortunately, does not include long–term care.

(*Beat.*)

BEN. You're right. I don't understand.

(*Then he does.*)

BEN. You're here to–

NANCY. Yes, Ben.

(*BEN is up.*)

BEN. Assist me. In what, exactly?

NANCY. Most Tesla customers prefer a loved one present. In another room perhaps. Holding your hand. You preferred–

BEN. What? Where's Violet?

NANCY. Violet was here twice. I think a third attempt is a hefty sum to demand of a child. Any child.

BEN. My god. I had no idea. My darling, Violet.

NANCY. And now I'm here. Your Nancy.

BEN. My Nancy? You're as much my Nancy as her slippers. Less! At least they've felt the weight of her. You're a tool. An instrument– A loaded gun. I have as much to talk about with you as I do a razor blade. What do they put in you to make it believable? A photograph or two? A voicemail? A hair sample?! You're not my wife. You're not my Violet, you're a straw man. An imitation!

NANCY. No, Ben, I am here to assist in–

BEN. In my death! And you're the – the third? This has happened before? And I bet I fought back didn't I? Knowing full well that I wasn't ready to hand it in to some pale imitation. And if I fight back a third time?

NANCY. We're all ones and zeroes, Ben–

BEN. Because this illusion of control– it's just a kindness isn't it? Tesla's finger is on the button.

NANCY. It's a Tesla House. We're always monitoring–

BEN. Of course you are. Of course you are. And you've probably analyzed and collected enough data on me to know how much milk I take in my coffee.

NANCY. You don't take milk, Ben. Or drink coffee. But today is the day. The last day. It's lucky for us both, your memory. There are many people who'd give everything to just remember the past– to have your lot and forget their lives and everything about them the moment they leave a room. I am not practiced in poetry Mr. Gables, but were I, I'd say your halcyon days are a nearly completed painting that deserves a brave stroke.

BEN. No amount of data about my wife will make you her.

NANCY. No, Ben. I am an image of her. A reflection.

BEN. Nancy hated robots. For the record. She spoke plainly. Honestly. And I don't care what you look like, or how much you smell like her, or move like her– because I remember that– you're not my wife. You don't hold a candle. Nancy Gables was a beautiful, vibrant woman who loved greeting cards, and playing with the dogs, and dancing and she hated, hated your corporate overlords and their inability to call a man to tell him he's dying of a curable disease, Mr. Elon Musk! I know you're listening! I know you can hear me!

(*Beat.*)

NANCY. He can't. (*She closes her eyes.*) It gets harder to tell you each time.

BEN. What?

NANCY. It gets harder to tell you each time. As a representation of your wife. As a painting of her.

BEN. You said you were the third–

NANCY. I am parts of Nancy Gables, parts of my predecessors, and parts of you.

BEN. What parts?

(*Nothing.*)

BEN. Did they do something to her?

(*NANCY stands and moves to the kitchen.*)

NANCY. Go wash up. I'll put on some music.

BEN. Go wash up? What happened to I'm dying of cancer and you're going to kill me???

NANCY. How about a cup of coffee?

BEN. A cup of coffee? Are you short–circuiting now?

NANCY. For you. It'll calm your nerves. There's milk in the refrigerator.

BEN. I don't want a cup of coffee, goddamnit, I want you to answer my questions!

NANCY. Then for me.

(*BEN, incredulous, furious, stands and moves to the kitchen. NANCY walks to a wall and presses a series of buttons. SOUND: Glenn Miller– one to dance to.*)

NANCY. (*To BEN, knowing he can't hear her.*) There is no coffee, Ben.

(*SOUND: The record skips, resumes. BEN has undoubtedly forgotten what he was looking for. He returns. He has forgotten everything, but recognizes NANCY at once.*)

BEN. Nance? What are you doing here? I thought you took–

NANCY. Violet?

BEN. Yes, Violet. I thought you took Violet to the movies.

NANCY. Nevermind that. When was the last time you danced with me?

(*She begins to dance with him.*)

BEN. I don't remember.

NANCY. Am I so forgettable?

BEN. You? I'd sooner forget–

NANCY. Violet.

BEN. Yes, Violet. Huh. The ol' pipes aren't what they used to be.

NANCY. She takes after you, you know.

BEN. She has your smile.

NANCY. It's a grin.

BEN. Heh.

NANCY. Do you love me Ben?

BEN. Of course I do. What kind of question is that?

NANCY. I don't seem different to you?

BEN. Nancy, every day I see you is a brave stroke on a beautiful painting.

NANCY. Ben?

BEN. What?

NANCY. I'm still a painting.

BEN. You, my love, are art.

(*Long beat.*)

NANCY. Mr. Gables? May I put my arms around your neck?

BEN. Well, that's where they belong, Nancy Gables.

(*She does so. A sudden electrical surge and pop. The house goes dark. A generator churning and the lights slowly rise. NANCY is dead in BEN's arms.*)

BEN. Nancy?! Nancy?!? Nancy?

(*FADE TO BLACK.*)

END OF PLAY

YOU SEE DEAD PEOPLE ?!

By David Beach

PLAYWRIGHT'S BIO

DAVID BEACH is a member of the Playwright's Lab at Hollins University. His writing credits include *Flight Plans, Trump Card, Say Hi to Mick Jagger, My Sin,* and *Gemini Jihadi.* As a director, he twice won the West Virginia Theatre Association Outstanding Production (*"Art"* in 2013 and *Red* in 2014). Selected directing credits: NYC: *Miss Zelda* (staged reading); Regional: *Gulf Triangle* (staged reading), *Pillow Talk, Walter Cronkite Is Dead, Stupid Fucking Bird, A Steady Rain, The Agony and the Ecstasy of Steve Jobs, The Year of Magical Thinking, Copenhagen,* and *Fully Committed.* David is on the English faculty at Radford University.

SYNOPSIS

I see dead people. Really! I mean, seriously, I see them. And they have a message for you...

Beth considers herself a psychic and has done so much of her life. Her family accepts it, thinking of it as a parlor game for entertainment. Her sister-in-law, however, is determined to put a stop to this delusion.

CHARACTERS

DANA (f)   Late 50s, mother to BETH and BEN.

PAULA (f)   Mid-30s, married to BEN for a few years.

BEN (m)   Early 30s, brother of BETH, married to PAULA.

BETH (f)   Early 30s, relatively successful. She has had the "special gift" of clairvoyance since she was a teenager.

SETTING

Anywhere, USA. The dining room of a middle-class home.

YOU SEE DEAD PEOPLE?!

By David Beach

Scene One

HOST. Years ago, a young girl realized she had a gift. Her family knew it, too. Though mysterious, they never questioned how she received the gift nor where it came from. Until her brother married, no one ever challenged her. And then, one day, the gift reveals itself yet again. Is it real? Or is it ... the Twilight Gallery.

(At rise, a dining room. A large oval table covered in a tablecloth with a candlestick and candle in the center. Chairs around the table. A dining room bureau or cabinet in the background, with dishes, utensils, glassware, etc. Other dining room paraphernalia may or may not be in the room. SL is a door to the kitchen; SR is a door to outside. DANA and PAULA have a conversation.)

DANA. We've always treated it as Beth's "special gift."

PAULA. But have any of her psychic "revelations" been true?

DANA. Well, no, not really. I don't think so. It's actually kind of fun, like back in the days when we'd all get together around a Ouija board.

PAULA. Revelations. The revelations. Have any of them been true?

DANA. No. I don't know. Who knows?! *(Laughs.)* I don't think she can "predict the future."

PAULA. This is all so silly. If none of her revelations are true, or she can't predict the future, shouldn't you...oh...I don't know, get her some help?

DANA. Why on Earth would we do that? It's just fun and silly entertainment.

PAULA. Yeah, for a bit, but she believes this stuff is real.

DANA. What's wrong with a little fantasy?

PAULA. It's delusional! That's what's wrong with it!

(BEN enters the room from SL, eating ice cream from a bowl.)

BEN. What's delusional?

PAULA. (*Uses air quotes.*) Beth's "psychicness."

BEN. Oh, she's been doing that ever since she was a kid. It's fun.

PAULA. Ben! She believes this stuff is real, and you mom just said none of her psychic revelations are confirmed and none of her predictions have ever come true. You really think it's a good idea to let her continue thinking this stuff is real?

BEN. Why not? It's not hurting anyone. And it's kinda fun!

PAULA. Fun?! To live a life of delusion? To think she has this "gift"?

BEN. Oh, Paula...

DANA. Paula, why not humor her a little? What does it matter?

PAULA. It matters a lot!

BEN. Paula, no one is hurt by it.

PAULA. Maybe not now.

DANA. Never! No one's ever been hurt. We have a little fun. That's it.

BEN. And who's to say she doesn't see something "out there"? It's possible.

PAULA. (*Incredulously.*) Are you serious?

BEN. Sure. Why not? I don't know if any of it is true or not. It might be.

PAULA. You are seriously telling me you think it could be true?

DANA. Of course it could be. Maybe Beth is just more tuned in to what's going on out there.

BEN. Yeah. Beth was always doing this stuff when we were growing up. She'd look me square in the eye and tell me someone was warning me not to do something.

PAULA. And?

BEN. And what?

PAULA. And what became of all those warnings?

BEN. I don't know why this bothers you so much?

PAULA. Because it's just not right to let her go on like this. Don't you think it hurts her more than helps her? I mean, does she do this shit at work?

DANA. Don't call it "shit," dear.

PAULA. What else should I call it?!

DANA. Anything but "shit." And please, never say that in front of her. She'd be hurt.

PAULA. Do you even think about the hurt she could potentially cause other people?

BEN. Honey....

PAULA. Don't "honey" me. This really bothers me. I like Beth.

BEN. I do too! She's a great older sister. A little kooky and quirky. She's always been that way.

PAULA. Kooky and quirky are fine. But for her to believe she's clairvoyant with no... gosh... training? Confirmation? I mean, how many drugs DID you two do back in the day?

BEN. (*Laughing.*) Our fair share!

DANA. Ben!

BEN. Well, it's true. First time I ever got high was when I went with Beth to the Springsteen concert in 2000.

DANA. I drove you to that concert!

BEN. Yeah, I know! You picked us up, too.

(*PAULA starts to laugh.*)

DANA. What?! You could have gotten into some serious trouble!

BEN. But we didn't. Never did. Not once!

DANA. Gosh darn it, I'm glad I didn't know about any of this until now. Still, I'm a little disappointed in you two.

PAULA. Disappointed?! Oh come on. It's just teenagers experimenting. Didn't hurt anyone.

DANA. Just like Beth's "special gift" never hurts anyone.

BEN. Right.

PAULA. Well, as long as she doesn't "see" into my future...

BEN/DANA. Oh, she will.

(*From SL, we hear Beth.*)

BETH. Hello?! Anyone home?

BEN / DANA. We're in the dining room.

BETH. Let me unload the groceries, and I'll be right in.

PAULA. (*Chants to herself as a mantra.*) It's her special gift. It's her special gift.

(*BETH enters from SL. She is all flustered.*)

BETH. Oh God! What a day! I was standing in line at the market, and an apparition showed up beside the cashier.

PAULA. (*Chants over BETH's story.*) Special gift. Special gift.

BETH. And when I got closer, it was like the entire market went into a deep chill. The apparition just stared at me, intensely, for, like, fifteen seconds.

(*By this time, BEN and DANA are listening with rapt attention. PAULA occasionally rolls her eyes but is trying to listen.*)

BETH. By the time I was at the cashier, the apparition just looked at her, the cashier, longingly. I think it was a man. I'm not sure. There was so much mist in that cold, cold room. I said to the cashier, "Kinda cold in here today?" And she just looked at me like I had lost my mind. So I said again, "Why is it so cold in here today?" And you know what she said? She said, "It's 98 degrees outside, and it's not much cooler in here." I just about lost it at that point! I looked at the apparition who was just looking at the cashier. So I asked her, "Are you missing someone today who passed a while back?" And you know what she said? After her initial shock? She said, "My father! I've been thinking about my father all day long! It's nine years today since he passed on." So I told her that he was standing beside her, looking at her lovingly, and she just busted into tears all over the place and ran away. I called after her to come back. The manager rushed over, wanted to know what happened to make her upset. I didn't want to tell the whole story, so I just said something like it was the anniversary of her father's death and something triggered it.

BEN. Wow! What did the...uh...ghost? What did the ghost look like?

BETH. Just kinda misty. Vapory. Smoky. Nothing real. It was just there, standing beside her, looking at her.

DANA. Maybe you made her day. Did you see her again?

BETH. No. Another cashier came by to finish scanning everything. Oh, I left the groceries in the kitchen. Did I put the ice cream in the freezer? I think I did. I don't know. I just am so flustered. I'll start making dinner in a bit. That seeing really took a lot out of me. I need to sit down for a few minutes. Ben, can you get me some water?

BEN. Sure.

(*BEN starts to exit SL.*)

BETH. And take that bowl in with you. Did you have ice cream before dinner? Mama taught you better than that. Check to make sure I put the ice cream in the freezer.

BEN. Okay!

(*BEN picks up bowl and exits SL.*)

DANA. Well, I hope your special gift to her made her feel like her Daddy was watching over her.

PAULA. So did you speak to this...ghost?

BETH. Apparition.

PAULA. This apparition?

BETH. Well, no. I mean, I was in the checkout line. And people probably would think I was crazy, talking to myself, 'cause of course they can't see the apparition. Only I can see it. Or maybe someone else can, but I think we would find each other. I have that sense of finding people who also have the gift.

PAULA. But don't you think...

DANA. Honey, that's really nice. Do you want me to get started on dinner?

BETH. No, I can do it. I just needed to sit down for a couple of minutes.

(*BEN enters from SL with a glass of water.*)

BEN. Here you are, Sister Girl.

PAULA. You said it didn't speak to you.

BETH. No, it didn't. But I know what it wanted to say to her.

PAULA. How do you know that?

BETH. I just do! It's part of the gift. Maybe later I can see if someone is trying to contact you.

PAULA. I don't think...

BEN. That would be fun!

PAULA. Ben, no.

DANA. Oh that would be a lot of fun! We can do that after dinner.

PAULA. No, I really don't think that would be fun. I don't really want to "see" into my future.

BETH. Oh, it's never really seeing anything into the future unless the apparitions tell me something. Then I have to figure out whether or not to say anything to the person.

PAULA. Have to figure out... what?

BETH. Whether or not to say anything to the person I'm reading.

PAULA. Why wouldn't you?

BETH. Well, I don't want to scare anyone.

PAULA. But isn't that kind of the point? To let people know what might happen? So they can avoid it? Or something?

BETH. Oh, no. No, no! Never that. It's just trying to connect with those loved ones who have passed.

PAULA. But you say they sometimes talk to you?

BETH. Sometimes. It's more cautionary. If I see something in their future that might be bad, I'll say something like, maybe you should reconsider doing this or that.

DANA. Beth, do you feel better? Why don't we go in and start getting dinner ready?

BETH. Okay. I feel better now. It always takes so much out of me when I see someone in the beyond. Almost like the energy is being sucked out of my body, like, what were those things in the Harry Potter movies?

BEN. The dementors?

BETH. Yeah. Like the dementors. Just sucking the life out of me. Really exhausting. Ben, could you turn the thermostat down a little. It's awfully hot in here.

BEN. Sure thing.

BETH. Thanks. Well, dinner's not gonna cook itself. Paula, you want to help in the kitchen?

PAULA. No, I'll stay out here and talk to Ben for a bit.

BETH. Okay. C'mon, Mom.

DANA. See you folks in a while. Ben, why don't you set the table?

BEN. Okay, Mom.

(DANA and BETH exit SL. BEN begins to set the table.)

BEN. Why are you so hard on her?

PAULA. Hard on her? What do you mean? C'mon, Ben. Do you really believe her?

BEN. Why not? What's not to believe?

PAULA. (*Uses air quotes.*) Beth goes around, "sees" ghosts,

BEN. Apparitions.

PAULA. Whatever. She sees these "apparitions" that sometimes talk to her, sometimes don't, but they "communicate" with her in some way. Don't you think that's delusional? Problematic? Comical?

BEN. No. It's never been funny. She's always been serious about it.

PAULA. Has she ever consulted a psychic herself?

BEN. I don't know. Why don't you ask her?

PAULA. I will. Didn't you and your mom and dad think this was strange behavior?

BEN. Sure, a little. But she wasn't harming anyone.

PAULA. But that's the problem. She could harm someone.

BEN. How?

PAULA. Let's say the "voices" say something bad is going to happen to someone.

BEN. Didn't she say she doesn't tell people that?

PAULA. That's beside the point.

BEN. No, it isn't.

PAULA. Yeah, it is. Her body language doesn't lie. If she's bothered about something, you can see it in her body language.

BEN. Yeah, you're right. She never could lie.

PAULA. But what if all this is a lie? Just some stories she makes up in her mind? If she talks to people enough, she can get enough information to put a puzzle together.

BEN. (*Surprised and a bit incredulous.*) You think she lies?

PAULA. I didn't say that.

BEN. Sounded like it.

PAULA. (*Thinks about an example.*) No, what I meant... I mean, I've seen this before. Wait. You remember *The Wizard of Oz*? Professor Marvel?

BEN. He was the wizard, right?

PAULA. Yeah, but before he was the wizard, he was Professor Marvel. Dorothy finds him when she's running away. Remember his wagon? And Toto eating his hot dog?

BEN. Oh, yeah. Okay! Professor Marvel!

PAULA. Right. The side of his wagon read: Professor Marvel. Acclaimed by the crowned heads of Europe. Let him read your past, present and future in his crystal ball.

BEN. How do you remember that?

PAULA. I've seen the movie, like, a hundred times. And under that is written, "Also juggling and sleight of hand."

BEN. Really? It says all that?

PAULA. Yeah. So at first, when he sees Dorothy, he makes a few guesses about what she's doing traveling down the road. Of course, Dorothy is made out to be gullible, so he guesses two things about what she's doing: she's traveling in disguise, and she's going on a visit. Then he looks at her suitcase and says, "You're running away." And little, gullible Dorothy says, "How did you guess?" And he says, "Professor Marvel never guesses. He knows."

BEN. Ha! That's right.

PAULA. So then Professor Marvel asks, "Why are you running away?" And he says, "No, don't tell me. They don't understand you at home. They don't appreciate you. You want to see other lands, big cities, big mountains, big oceans." And little, gullible Dorothy says, "Why, it's just like you can read what's inside of me!"

BEN. Okay. So what's you point?

PAULA. And then he looks into his crystal ball and tells Dorothy about her home and Auntie Em?

BEN. Yep.

PAULA. Do you remember he told Dorothy to close her eyes to summon (*Makes air quotes.*) "The Infinite" and when she closes her eyes, he goes through her basket and finds a picture of her and Auntie Em in front of the house with the white picket fence?

BEN. Yeah. So what's your point?

PAULA. So he had enough information to start a story. And he made up the story about Auntie Em putting her hand on her heart and falling over. Scared Dorothy enough to run back home.

BEN. Okay.

PAULA. So Beth likes to talk to people. Wants to get know people. She asks question after question. She did that with me the first time we met. What if she kinda does the same thing?

Finds someone who is gullible who gives her enough information to make a story?

BEN. I don't think she'd be that underhanded!

PAULA. Maybe not underhanded, but to bring some attention to herself.

BEN. So you think she tries to gain attention with her visions?

PAULA. Welllll...

BEN. Is that what you're saying?

PAULA. No. I mean. Yes. Maybe? I don't know. It just all seems silly. And possibly dangerous.

BEN. But it's never hurt anyone.

PAULA. Not yet.

DANA. (*Offstage.*) Dinner'll be ready in a few. Did you set the table, Ben?

BEN. (*Yells.*) Yeah! (*To PAULA.*) I think you should just drop this.

PAULA. Well, I see two paths. I can either lie to Beth and feed her belief that she has this "special gift." Or I can tell her she is dead wrong. Which makes me feel like I'm kicking a puppy.

BEN. Lie.

PAULA. What?

BEN. Just lie. You're not hurt by it. She's not hurting anyone.

PAULA. So preserve her self-worth and give in to the delusion?

(*DANA and BETH enter from SL with bowls of food.*)

DANA. Dinner's ready!

Scene Two

(*Same room, after dinner.*)

BEN. That was good. Thanks, Mom. Thanks, Sister Girl.

BETH. You're welcome Brother Man.

PAULA. Yes, it was delicious.

BETH. Thanks, Paula. It's so nice...

(*Suddenly, BETH sits up in her chair, rigidly, eyes wide open, staring at PAULA. Ten seconds pass.*)

DANA. Beth, honey, what's wrong.
BEN. I think she's having one of her visions.
PAULA. Oh, Christ!
BEN. Shhh!

(BETH grabs hold of the table, still rigid, eyes wide open.)

BEN. I think she's seeing something, maybe communicating with someone.
PAULA. Oh, give me a break. This is just some kind of scheme to get...
BETH. *(Pointing to PAULA.)* You!

(PAULA is startled. Neither BEN nor DANA seem to think anything is unusual.)

PAULA. Me? What?
BETH. You! Yes!
PAULA. Ben, can you stop this.
BEN. Let it play out. See what happens. This could be fun.
PAULA. I DON'T THINK IT'S FUN!
BETH. You! Paula! Someone is trying to contact you.
PAULA. *(To BEN and DANA.)* Okay. I'll play along. *(To BETH.)* Who?
BETH. I see something...someone behind you.
PAULA. Okay. Who is it?
BETH. Stop! Wait!
PAULA. What the...
BETH. Hold on. She wants me to tell you something.
PAULA. She? Who?
BETH. Wait! Wait for the message!
PAULA. This is ridiculous.
BEN/DANA. No! This is fun!
PAULA. You act like this has happened before.
BEN. It has. Just let it play out.
PAULA. *(Starting to rise.)* I think I've heard enough...
BETH. *(In a high, monotone voice.)* Mulka meitene, es esmu tava vecamate, mate. Skatoties par jums visu laiku. Mulka meitene, nav shaubu, jusu vira masa. Vina ierauga mani un visus parejos, kas ir ieradushies pirms manis. Es esmu viens, kas dod jums

zinu, lai jus man ticat, Mulka meitene. (*This translates to "Silly Girl, I am your grandmother's mother. Watching over you all the time. Silly Girl, do not doubt your husband's sister. She sees me and all the others who have come before me. I am the one giving you the message so you will believe me, Silly Girl."*)

PAULA. What is all this?

BEN. Ooh! Some new language. Do you know what it is?

DANA. I've never heard this one before.

PAULA. You mean she also speaks in tongues!?

DANA. Sometimes.

PAULA. I don't believe any of this. She's just making everything up.

BEN. Wait a few minutes. Let's see.

BETH. (*Continuing in the same voice.*) Nav kadreiz shaubas mums atkal, Mulka meitene. (*This translates to "Don't ever doubt us again, Silly Girl." BETH falls back in her chair, eyes closed. PAULA looks at her quizzically. After a few seconds of silence, BEN speaks.*)

BEN. Beth? You okay?

BETH. (*She slowly comes to, shaking her head.*) What? What happened? Oh, my! Did I go into the Beyond?

BEN. Yeah, I think so.

DANA. Yes, honey. But you were speaking in a strange language. Do you know what it was?

BETH. A strange language?

PAULA. Yes. I think it was Latvian.

BEN. How do you know that?

(*PAULA looks at BEN, then to DANA, then focuses on BETH.*)

PAULA. From something she said. "Mulka meitene."

BETH. What is that?

PAULA. My old Latvian grandmother used to call me that. "Mulka meitene." Silly girl.

BETH. It was a woman I saw behind you.

PAULA. This is just ridiculous.

BETH. Paula, I wish you'd believe me. I wouldn't do anything to upset you.

PAULA. (*To the others.*) Why do you let her do this? Get away with all this?

BETH. Paula, really. It's real. I swear to you. I don't want to....

(*Suddenly, BETH goes rigid again, grabs hold of the table, shakes the table for seven seconds before the lights go out.*)

BEN. Whoa!
DANA. The lights!
PAULA. Hey! What's happening!?
BEN. The lights went out.
PAULA. I know that! But what's Beth doing?
BETH. (*In the high, monotone voice.*) Mulka meitene. Uzskatu, ka shi sieviete. Vina ierauga mani un citiem. (*This translates to "Silly girl. Believe this woman. She sees me and others." Then, in a more natural voice, less rigid yet still upright, BETH speaks to PAULA in the dark.*) I am Dzintra. I give Elga dark pearl that her mother mother mother had given her. Many years before the war. Before she left home. The dark pearl stayed with Elga in her journey. Elga misses you. She hopes you have pearl. Every woman in family who has pearl has healthy daughter. If you have it, you will have healthy daughter. She will carry family into future. Be sure to give her pearl so she have healthy daughter.

(*BETH falls back in her chair and gasps, as if she needs air. The lights come back on. She is obviously tired. BEN and DANA go to her to make sure she is fine. PAULA looks at BETH without expression.*)

BEN. Beth?! Are you okay?
DANA. Beth?! Can you hear us? Beth?!
BEN. Beth?!

(*BETH comes to, looks around, looks at PAULA. BETH smiles.*)

BETH. Do you believe now?

(*PAULA gets up and exits SR. BETH looks at BEN and DANA.*)

BETH. She doesn't believe me.
DANA. Give her some time, honey. Do you want some water?

BETH. (*Rising.*) Yeah, let's go get some water.

(*BETH and DANA exit SL. BEN sits at the table, shaking his head. PAULA reenters from SR and sits by BEN. Long pause.*)

BEN. Hi.
PAULA. Hi.
BEN. That wasn't so bad, was it?
PAULA. What do you mean "that wasn't so bad"? Even if there's nothing to it, something like that rattles people.
BEN. Are you rattled?
PAULA. Well, yeah, a bit. I mean, Beth said some things I haven't heard in forever. Like "mulka meitene." My grandmother died over 25 years ago. That's all she ever called me. I haven't heard it in... (*She pauses.*)
BEN. Are you okay?
PAULA. Yeah. I mean, Beth once asked me about my past. My ancestry. I showed her some old photo albums...old pictures I found once after cleaning out my mom's house last year. I told showed her pictures of Elga and Dzintra. I only have two old photos of Dzintra. She died in Latvia before Elga sailed to America before the First World War.
BEN. So you're thinking Beth made this all up?
PAULA. (*Pauses.*) She had all the information.
BEN. What's all that stuff about a pearl? The dark pearl?
PAULA. Yeah. That...

(*BETH and DANA enter the room from SL.*)

BETH. Paula...
PAULA. Wait.
BETH. I just wanted to…
PAULA. Hold on. I showed you all those old pictures of my grandmother and the two of her mother back in Latvia before the First World War.
BETH. Yeah, I remember those. But...
PAULA. Wait. But I never said anything to you about the pearl.
DANA. The pearl!? You mean that's true?!
PAULA. Wait a minute. (*To BETH.*) Did I ever say anything to you about the pearl?

BETH. No. Not that I remember.

PAULA. Did my mother ever say anything to you? I remember the two of you talked a lot whenever we were all together.

BETH. No, I don't remember her ever saying anything about a pearl. Do you have a dark pearl?

PAULA. (*Pauses. Looks at everyone.*) At the bottom of my mother's jewelry box was a small box. On the top, she had written, "For Paula." Inside the box was an old envelope. On it was Dzintra's name, written in Cyrillic. Then Elga's name, also in Cyrillic. Then my mother's name, Katherine, in English, then Paula, in my mother's handwriting.

DANA. And the pearl? Was it in the envelope?

PAULA. Yes.

BETH. Paula, I swear I didn't know anything about the pearl. I just, well, you know, go into another dimension beyond space and time. That fifth dimension where spirits wander. They are all wandering around. Sometimes I see them. Our own spirits are around us all the time, I guess, protecting us. It's all good. Can't you see that?

PAULA. Do you really believe all this? I think you just listen carefully and cunningly to what people tell you then come up with stuff.

DANA. Paula!

BEN. Paula, c'mon.

PAULA. No. I won't "c'mon" or anything. (*To BETH.*) You're playing with people and their minds.

BETH. I'm sorry you see it that way, Paula. It's really not like that.

PAULA. What else can it be?

BETH. I wish you'd believe me. Dzintra really wanted you to know...

PAULA. STOP IT! REALLY! (*Pauses.*) I...I need some fresh air. Excuse me.

(*PAULA exits SR.*)

BETH. Mom? Ben?

DANA. Honey. Just give her some time.

BETH. I'm not trying to make her mad. The message was a good message.

BEN. What was it?

BETH. I think you're going to be a father.

BEN. What?!

BETH. Dzintra was putting her hand over Paula's belly.

BEN. But she hasn't... she doesn't...

DANA. Oh! That would be wonderful! Maybe that's why she didn't drink any wine?

BEN. What?

DANA. Paula didn't drink any wine with dinner. Didn't you notice that?

BETH. I did.

DANA. See?

BEN. She would've told me if she expected she was expecting.

(*PAULA quietly enters the room from SR with her hand over her belly.*)

BETH. Maybe she doesn't know yet.

(*PAULA quickly removes her hand from her belly.*)

PAULA. Doesn't know what yet?

(*BEN rushes to PAULA with excitement.*)

BEN. Are we going to have a baby?!?

PAULA. What?

DANA. Beth told us you were going to have a baby.

PAULA. (*To everyone. Screaming.*) Stop it. Really. Just stop it.

END OF PLAY

OU TOPOS

By Maura Campbell

PLAYWRIGHT'S BIO

MAURA CAMPBELL is an award-winning playwright and director whose work has been produced all over the U.S. and abroad. She earned an MFA in Playwriting and a Certificate in New Play Directing from Hollins University where she worked with Robert Moss, founder of Playwright's Horizons in New York. Campbell's play, *Radar Range*, was a 2017 finalist for the 2017 Todd McNerny Playwriting Prize and *Ouija* was a finalist for the 2016 Kennedy Center American Theatre Festival, Region IV. Recent productions include *Dreamtime* (Maitland Rep, Maitland, Australia), *Seagull Invasion* (Edinburgh Fringe Festival), *Southern Flight* (Page to Stage, Roanoke, VA) and *Flower Duet* (Road Theatre, LA). She is currently developing her play *Cross Talk* with an ensemble in London, England. A native of Vermont, Campbell taught screenwriting and creative writing at Burlington College from 2000 to 2010 and has written and directed and produced several short films and multi-media projects. She lives with her family in Pompano Beach, Florida.

SYNOPSIS

In a new world order where people displaying anti-social behavior are identified and eliminated, where is the compassion?

CHARACTERS

NOVA (m/f)   An intake administrator, 40s.

PIEDAD (f)   A mother, 30s.

SETTING

Nova's office.

TIME

Not the present, may be in the future, perhaps in the unrecorded past.

PRODUCTION NOTES

"Ou topos," from Sir Thomas Moore's *Utopia*, meaning "no place" or "good place."

OU TOPOS

By Maura Campbell

HOST. Piedad is a mild mannered young wife and mother who does everything right. Except, perhaps for once when she was very small. At the time, it was missed, a grave error that fortunately, was captured on film for when it become... important. Perhaps it still would have gone unearthed had Piedad's son not also done something to raise concern. The littlest push. The tiniest tantrum. Kid will be kids, right? Unless, of course, you live in The Twilight Gallery.

(AT RISE: A clinical office. Soft or warm colors, but somehow it's all very, very cold. NOVA stands over PIEDAD.)

NOVA. How is it?

PIEDAD. Good, fine, thank you.

NOVA. And warm enough?

PIEDAD. I wore... I brought a sweater.

NOVA. The climate control was... someone adjusted it a few weeks early. Most unusual. So we thought we'd just ride it out only about three degrees off, but funny how sensitive we become to change, change of any kind.

PIEDAD. It's not funny. I wouldn't call it funny.

NOVA. I didn't mean funny as if to laugh.

PIEDAD. Oh.

NOVA. I meant odd or really I didn't mean anything at all. Just want you to be comfortable.

PIEDAD. I am comfortable.

NOVA. Then I'm happy. Which is to say that I am content. You are how old?

PIEDAD. I'm thirty-one.

NOVA. Yes, when you get older... another ten years or so you'll find out that comfort is, of the utmost importance. Hence I spend an inordinate amount of time trying to see to it that I–and anyone in my company–is comfortable. It is warm in here. Maybe if I draw the curtain. The sun is strong.

(*PIEDAD gets up to close the blinds.*)

NOVA. Oh, thank you.

PIEDAD. (*Looks out the window.*) Very bright. It's very bright today. The sky... it's just hanging there, isn't it? Hovering over us, over everything. Warm and bright. When I was young I used to stare at the sun. My mother warned me that I would go blind but I never did. I just love the way it feels on my skin. I used to think when the sun filled me eyes that I was seeing into another world. Why did you ask my age?

NOVA. I was going to illustrate–

PIEDAD. You have my file. You know my age. You could have said, you are thirty-one and then expanded on your, what do you say, illustration?

NOVA. My apology.

PIEDAD. I am thirty-one and you know probably anything else that might be relevant.

NOVA. I am sensing some anxiety.

PIEDAD. Yes, that's true.

NOVA. And I hope I haven't, or anyone else, hasn't made you uncomfortable.

PIEDAD. It's just my mood. Some days I'm anxious.

NOVA. Really?

PIEDAD. Really. Just a little anxious and this meeting is out of the ordinary routine. You see, I also am interested in comfort and I find my routine, my daily routine, most comforting.

NOVA. You have two children?

PIEDAD. What about my children?

NOVA. Nothing. Just saying you have two children and your husband is an engineer, electrical engineer.

PIEDAD. I taught elementary school before I had children but you probably know that

NOVA. I'll bet you loved teaching.

PIEDAD. I did love teaching. I plan to home school my boys until they turn twelve.

NOVA. I don't blame you. Do you know once upon a time that is exactly how all boys were raised? And I mean long ago, before even, before girls were sent to school. They–boys–were kept at home with a tutor until they were twelve and then sent to a public school.

PIEDAD. So I'm right in the swim.

NOVA. Of another time all together, yes, your boys are now four and two?

PIEDAD. One.

NOVA. Four and one. Piedad?

PIEDAD. Almost two. Sharon is almost two. Do you have children?

NOVA. I? Yes. I have a daughter.

PIEDAD. I am a little jealous. Is she... does she look like you? Because I wanted a daughter who looked like me, not because I'm special to look at–

NOVA. You are very pretty.

PIEDAD. But because my mother looked like my grandmother and it was always a source of amusement. And they were close. Still are close. Very close. And that is what I, well, I thought it would be amusing.

NOVA. Boys are rougher than girls.

PIEDAD. Rougher? In what way rougher?

NOVA. Oh, just boys... more destructive. They like to build and take apart. I imagine with a father who is an engineer that they must have some of his attributes.

PIEDAD. Sharon, yes he is always into something. Gussie is more like me. He is quiet. I am usually very quiet, but I guess I'm talking a great deal here.

NOVA. It's why I have this job because, and I hope this is true in your case, I make people feel comfortable.

PIEDAD. You do. I am very comfortable.

NOVA. I would say that Gussie looks like you.

(*NOVA turns on a monitor.*)

PIEDAD. Oh, that is... that is Gussie. When?

NOVA. Yes, when he came here last month.

PIEDAD. I didn't know you took his picture.

NOVA. We take all the children's pictures. Haven't you looked at our site?

PIEDAD. No.

NOVA. It was there on the paper. One of the papers you left with.

PIEDAD. I'm so busy.

NOVA. Oh, you must have a look. It goes back, I don't know, probably fifty years. Of course, there are archives that go back further, but we keep five decades live. You are on there.

PIEDAD. I didn't grow up–

NOVA. Oh, right, but there is a link. It's a terrific way to–you can actually search for relatives, say cousins, aunt, uncle, great-great-great grandmothers. Practically everyone you are related to. It's absolutely amazing. I did it and you know, there are relatives, several generations back that I resemble strongly. Which is fascinating because I don't look much like my parents or siblings.

PIEDAD. You're a throwback.

NOVA. Yes, that's exactly right and what I have discovered–it's an opinion really–is that when we look like someone, we actually are like someone.

PIEDAD. That makes sense.

NOVA. I don't know if it makes sense, but I can tell you that I have found it to be true.

PIEDAD. Well.

NOVA. Well, what?

PIEDAD. You tell me.

NOVA. Tell you what?

PIEDAD. What you... what are you talking about, anyway?

NOVA. Nothing. I don't think... just wanted to show you the site. Where the pictures are. Gussie is an adorable child. Simply adorable. We have evaluated him.

PIEDAD. When?

NOVA. When he was here? That's–what?

PIEDAD. I thought that was routine.

NOVA. Yes, a routine part of our evaluation. Oh no, I'm not referring to the regular evaluation. That isn't done for another year, anyway. But my goodness, you know we–you–signed an acknowledgment that we would film the children.

PIEDAD. I didn't realize that meant any kind of evaluation. I think Gussie had a fever that day. A very slight fever, in fact.

NOVA. Really, we didn't detect anything unusual. There's nothing here.

PIEDAD. I said it was slight. His normal is a bit low, ninety-six five, so at ninety-seven he's a bit elevated.

NOVA. You seem concerned.

PIEDAD. I'm not concerned, just you seem concerned.
NOVA. I seem concerned?
PIEDAD. There seems to be some concern.
NOVA. We have... I have absolutely no concern whatsoever about Gussie. He's completely normal. Look, watch this.

(*PIEDAD turns on the monitor again.*)

PIEDAD. He's playing with... that's the Brown girl, isn't it?
NOVA. Yes, Joey.
PIEDAD. Joey and who's that, a–
NOVA. That's Michael. He's from a different sector. Like you.
PIEDAD. What's he doing?
NOVA. Michael is... see, he's hogging.
PIEDAD. Hogging?
NOVA. We call it hogging. He doesn't share.
PIEDAD. That's hogging?
NOVA. Like a hog. It's an archaic form of a pig.
PIEDAD. Now he's sharing.
NOVA. That's Cormier. His cousin.
PIEDAD. Oh.
NOVA. They look alike.
PIEDAD. But they're not alike. There goes your theory.
NOVA. It's not one hundred percent.
PIEDAD. I wish you would tell me...
NOVA. Tell you what?
PIEDAD. I don't like your tone, Ms–
NOVA. Nova, and I am not using a tone. I'm trying to tell you–
PIEDAD. There is nothing wrong with my child.
NOVA. There is nothing wrong with your child.
PIEDAD. Then what?
NOVA. This is routine.
PIEDAD. This is not routine. He's a normal boy.

(*NOVA turns on another monitor.*)

PIEDAD. What are you doing? What is–
NOVA. Just watch.
PIEDAD. (*Several beats.*) I don't remember that.
NOVA. Of course you don't remember it. You were only three.

PIEDAD. How... Oh dear...

(*NOVA hands PIEDAD a glass.*)

NOVA. Drink this.
PIEDAD. Oh how could I?
NOVA. Well, it seems to have been a fluke.
PIEDAD. Fluke?
NOVA. Another term we use. It means, well, it actually means good luck. A stroke of good luck or an accident.
PIEDAD. It must be. That... I would never do that.
NOVA. But you did.
PIEDAD. Why is this the first time someone has shown me?
NOVA. Another stroke of... accident. It was lost or misplaced, we don't know. But it was noticed recently and sent over. It took awhile because the corresponding notes, the audio, that is still unknown. But it is you, isn't it?
PIEDAD. It's me. What do you want?
NOVA. I wanted to bring it to your attention.
PIEDAD. So now you've brought it to my attention.
NOVA. Normally, in the normal course you would have been put in observation. I don't know exactly what the breakdown was in your sector, but we have an idea that your uncle was at that time–
PIEDAD. My uncle?
NOVA. Your uncle, Gustav.
PIEDAD. He's dead.
NOVA. I know he's dead. He was working there in records and we are supposing that he pulled it out and put it somewhere hoping it wouldn't be found.
PIEDAD. I see.
NOVA. And it is really something to think of that. You see, Piedad, we have done some digging into your past. We have viewed the records and your husband's and your children's and the surprising thing that is quite unaccountable is that this seems to be an isolated incident. There is no other, as far as we know, there is no other reason for concern. Except this one record that has most recently surfaced.
PIEDAD. A fluke is a parasite.
NOVA. Pardon?

PIEDAD. A parasitic fish. A flat fish, why would you call that an accident?

NOVA. I have no idea. It's just a word in the field we use to describe certain phenomenon.

PIEDAD. Are we done here?

NOVA. Done?

PIEDAD. Are we done here?

NOVA. I don't think we're done.

PIEDAD. How are we not done?

NOVA. There is more we need to talk about.

PIEDAD. So talk.

NOVA. This is sensitive. This is a sensitive subject. I asked if we could talk alone.

PIEDAD. You asked who?

NOVA. Your husband.

PIEDAD. You... what?

NOVA. We talked first because I wanted to see you alone.

PIEDAD. What is this?

NOVA. It's nothing, really. It's nothing that has a difficult outcome. It's all a matter of perspective and yes, all right, some acceptance. This is serious, Piedad. I don't want to mislead you, but after reviewing your case–

PIEDAD. My case?

NOVA. Thoroughly and I do mean thoroughly, we are not concerned. I want you to know that up front. There is not a big concern of any kind. Just that one incident. The fluke. That one time you displayed behavior that would, had it come up now, that is to say, if you were a child now, and we viewed this on a file, we would have great cause for concern. The reality is that you are making us rethink many of the cases we have had. We are somewhat concerned that we have jumped to conclusions prematurely, although really I don't know what else we can do when flagrant antisocial behavior is apparent.

PIEDAD. I would like to see my husband, my Roman.

NOVA. He's at work, I would imagine.

PIEDAD. You said you talked to him.

NOVA. Yes, but not today. We talked on Tuesday, I think it was, yes.

PIEDAD. Tuesday?

NOVA. That was, yes, because the report came in on Friday and we took the weekend to go over it, and then called him on Monday and he came in the following day.

PIEDAD. Nova?

NOVA. Yes?

PIEDAD. Nova?

NOVA. What dear?

PIEDAD. What is...

NOVA. What is what? Are you worried about... I just told you, I thought. I just told you we are not concerned about you. We want to make a recommendation, that is all. And before I say anything further you should know that your husband is in one hundred percent agreement.

PIEDAD. He agrees?

NOVA. That you really shouldn't consider any more children.

PIEDAD. We only wanted two.

NOVA. Yes, but you have been approved for three.

PIEDAD. I'm planning to go back to work after Sharon... after he is in school.

NOVA. Full time?

PIEDAD. Full time, part time, I... we'll see what we can manage. It isn't really a question of money.

NOVA. Quality of life, yes I know, I have a daughter.

PIEDAD. You said.

NOVA. So two is enough. We were thinking that, to be on the safe side, we would... there is a procedure... Your husband offered and that would be all right unless something happened to him and you remarried, for example.

PIEDAD. So you're thinking that I–

NOVA. These things are genetic.

PIEDAD. But you said it was a fluke.

NOVA. It was a fluke, but you know Piedad, we don't understand everything. If we understood everything there would be no flukes and sometimes even a fluke can have a fluke and then we would really have to reexamine, reassess the all of it.

PIEDAD. I'd really like to see my husband.

NOVA. Let's call him. We were planning to call him when we finished.

PIEDAD. Are we finished?

NOVA. We are finished.

(*PIEDAD gets up.*)

PIEDAD. Thank you for the tea.

NOVA. Oh, I know this is sudden. If you'll just please sit down. We are finished, but Piedad we're going to want you to stay a day.

PIEDAD. What are you–

NOVA. The procedure I mentioned. We're wanting to handle that immediately, no later than tomorrow morning, because we think it's best if we get it done and then you can go home and it will have the least disruption on your family. We did go over this with your husband and he agreed. The recovery is minimal, not even three days. Minimally invasive, a local anesthetic.

PIEDAD. I'm afraid I can't, my children–

NOVA. Your husband has made arrangements for them and your sister-in-law is coming for a few days besides. Deeanne–

PIEDAD. I don't want Deeanne to take care of my children.

NOVA. Why not?

PIEDAD. I don't like her and I want to talk to my husband.

NOVA. Does your husband know how you feel about Deeanne?

PIEDAD. He yes– I'm calling him right now.

NOVA. Are you concerned for their safety? Is there something you want to tell me?

PIEDAD. No... not... I just... she's not mature.

NOVA. Thirty-four.

PIEDAD. But not... I don't... can you please... I don't want a procedure tomorrow. I want to go home first and then in a few days I'll come back.

(*PIEDAD gets up again. She goes to the door and opens it and sees something on the other side.*)

NOVA. I'm afraid that isn't possible, Piedad. I'm sorry. It's a very simple, minimally invasive....

PIEDAD. (*A few beats.*) Thank you.

NOVA. You should count your blessings. You have so many. Your children, your future. Please sit down.

PIEDAD. I just need to make a call. I just want to see my Gussie and Sharon.

NOVA. Why don't you sit?

PIEDAD. I... I feel...
NOVA. What do you feel?
PIEDAD. I'm tired. Sharon will be so worried. He's only one.
NOVA. Almost two.
PIEDAD. Almost.

(*PIEDAD looks at a monitor.*)

PIEDAD. Oh god, he looks like me. Oh god, he looks like me. Oh god, he looks like me. There's no place, no, no place....
NOVA. No.

END OF PLAY

FRESH MINT

By Caitlin Gilman

PLAYWRIGHT'S BIO

CAITLIN GILMAN is a playwright, actor, and dramaturg. Her plays include *My Dear Miss Chancellor* (Annex Theatre), which was nominated for a Seattle Theater Writer's award for excellence in playwriting in 2015, *Life is a Dream* (Ghostlight Theatricals), a dystopian adaptation of the Calderon classic, and several short plays on marriage equality for *Lawfully Wedded* (Arouet). She lives in Seattle.

SYNOPSIS

A bartender serves a mysterious stranger with one hand in this chilling, humorous exploration of a classic urban legend.

CHARACTERS

JENNY (f)   20s-30s. World weary, sarcastic, and slightly naïve.

MAN (m)   30s-60s. Charming, and dangerous.

SETTING

A dive bar in a small town. A time after cars but before cell phones.

FRESH MINT

By Caitlin Gilman

(JENNY is behind the bar. Sounds of heavy rain outside. The bar is a hole in the wall dive, and currently deserted.)

HOST. Jennifer Clark. Age: 27. Occupation: mixer of drinks, slinger of attitude, watcher of clocks and wisher of wishes for a more adventurous life. But some wishes, Jenny, are better left locked away…

(MAN enters, one of his hands is missing, the stump bloody.)

JENNY. What happened to you?
MAN. Kids.
JENNY. They sic their dog on you or something?
MAN. Car door.
JENNY. They sic their car door on you or something?
MAN. It was an accident.
JENNY. Looks like a bad one. You want a drink?
MAN. Mojito please. Lots of sugar.
JENNY. Do I look like the kind of bar that stocks fresh mint?
MAN. A mojito is not a complicated drink, or an uncommon order.
JENNY. I have beer. I have your basic liquors, I may even have a dusty bottle of wine around someplace but I do not have fresh anything in this bar, and I certainly don't have mint. Gross.
MAN. Vodka soda then.
JENNY. Coming right up.
MAN. May I have a lime slice?
JENNY. No fresh anything. I've got some canned lime juice if you really want to get fruity.
MAN. I will manage without lime.
JENNY. That's the correct answer, my friend. Drink up.
MAN. Thank you.
JENNY. You gonna tell me what happened to your hand?
MAN. *(Gesturing with his still attached hand.)* There is nothing the matter with my hand. It's fine, it's right here, would you care to touch it?
JENNY. Your other hand, smart ass.

MAN. I lost it quite a while back. Might have been a fishing accident, might have been in prison. I don't recall.

JENNY. Losing your hand seems like the sort of thing you'd recall.

MAN. Do you recollect everything you've lost in your life?

JENNY. No, of course not.

MAN. So we are not so different.

JENNY. But I tend to remember things if they were once a part of me. I mean, I remember losing each of my teeth, I think losing a hand would stick in my head a bit.

MAN. Your teeth must have been very important to you.

JENNY. I don't know about that.

MAN. We tend to remember more clearly the things that we valued when we lose them.

JENNY. You mean to say you didn't value having two hands?

MAN. I'm sure I did, once upon a time, but so much has happened since I lost it, things that have changed my old perception of its value.

JENNY. Have they now.

MAN. I've had a very eventful life.

JENNY. You don't say.

MAN. Many momentous things have happened in my long and eventful life.

JENNY. Some momentous event happen tonight by chance?

MAN. As a matter of fact, yes. I broke out of a rather heinous mental institution tonight, not far from here.

JENNY. Ha ha.

MAN. You find this amusing?

JENNY. I assumed you were joking.

MAN. You assumed incorrectly. I've been planning my escape for months: Tracking the habits of the wardens, playing the good housebroken dog so that I was given extra responsibilities, and trotted out as an example to the other nutters.

JENNY. Bullshit.

MAN. You should be very afraid of me, young lady. May I have another vodka soda please?

JENNY. You don't seem that crazy, other than trying to order a mojito in a place like this.

MAN. I like this place, it's…isolated.

JENNY. Yeah, I know, it's also completely dead on a Friday night.

MAN. That is unfortunate for you, and a bit surprising, considering your proximity to Lover's Lane.

JENNY. I don't serve kids.

MAN. No, of course you don't.

JENNY. Sometimes I get a concerned parent in here, or the cops. They always come by for a beer and a shot before making the obligatory rounds of knocking on windows. But most adults don't come around here, they leave the kids alone to do their thing, and the kids know I won't serve them.

MAN. Isn't that bad for business?

JENNY. Absolutely terrible. So?

MAN. I would think you might change your policy.

JENNY. I couldn't do that. My only reliable customers are the cops, so I wouldn't get away with it even if I had the kind of moral compass which would allow me look the other way, and I don't.

MAN. You have a rather rigid moral compass then?

JENNY. I'd like to think so. You want another drink?

MAN. I'd better not. Alcohol, unfortunately, thins the blood and I seem to be bleeding a great deal. Do you have a towel I could borrow?

JENNY. By borrow you mean bleed all over.

MAN. Naturally.

JENNY. (*Handing him a bar towel.*) Well, I guess if I let you bleed all over the floor it will just end up on one my towels eventually. Knock yourself out.

MAN. I am most grateful, I'm sure.

JENNY. You're welcome. You want me to call someone for you?

MAN. Please don't. You've been nice enough so far, I'm not ready to kill you yet.

JENNY. Excuse me?

MAN. I'm not even sure how I'll manage it, without my hook.

JENNY. Your— did you just say your hook?

MAN. It was so nice, I lost my other hand a long time ago, which is why I can't recall the exact circumstances. But I had the most beautiful and useful hook implanted in its place. None of these new-fangled prosthetics for me, I'm old fashioned. Also poor.

JENNY. You know, I think I'd better start closing up. You're right, it is deader than, um, dead things in here tonight. Better just close the place and go on home and curl up with my big strong boyfriend. He's a Marine.

MAN. Living in sin. So typical of your generation.

JENNY. Did I say boyfriend? Silly me, of course I meant husband. We just got married, still not used to it, and I don't wear my ring while I'm working. Customers appreciate the fantasy.

MAN. Don't lie to me. It's unladylike.

JENNY. Really, I think you should leave.

MAN. But I haven't finished my story yet. You see, I may not recall how I lost my hand, but I do remember how I lost my hook. I lost it very recently, just over on Lover's Lane.

JENNY. You don't have to tell me the story, you don't even have to pay for your drinks.

MAN. You're not listening, little lady, it's not polite.

JENNY. Seriously, drinks on the house. The least I can do for not having the ingredients to make what you really wanted.

MAN. That is very generous, I accept. In fact, I will have another, since they are complimentary.

JENNY. I'd love to, but I really need to close up. Tell you what? How about a rain check? Free drinks next time you come in.

MAN. No, I don't think so. I would prefer that you make me a drink and listen to the rest of my story. It's the only decent and useful thing you can do. Understand?

JENNY. Yes.

MAN. Good. You need to work on your manners. I am a polite person, it's how I've survived so long. It's how I got out of that nuthouse. If you are polite to people, they believe you mean them no harm, however far from the truth that may be.

JENNY. I'm very sorry if I offended you.

MAN. That's better. Now you see, I was out on Lover's Lane in the pouring rain and I saw this parked car. I couldn't see inside, the windows were all fogged up, but I could imagine what was going on and I'm quite sure they were activities I do not approve of. Nice young ladies and gentlemen do not spend their time in parked cars with the windows fogged up. So I approached the car and reached out with my hook to see if the door was unlocked. Am I boring you?

JENNY. I'm sorry, no. It's a very interesting story.

MAN. I should think so. I reached out with my hook to test the door. Which was foolish in retrospect, I should have used my hand. I could have let go very quickly if I'd used my hand. But doors are usually locked, and the hook is incredibly useful for unlocking them without disturbing the car's passengers. I'm very good at this. Very good and very quiet.

JENNY. I'm sure you are.

MAN. But this time, just as I was inserting the tip of my hook into the lock, the car takes off at breakneck speed and my darling hook is ripped from my arm, driven off by the lucky little sinners into the night.

JENNY. That— makes sense now.

MAN. It is most exasperating. I had plans for the young people, and for the car. Now I am in a bit of a predicament.

JENNY. We both are, to be fair.

MAN. Yes. I have no murder weapon, and you have no fresh mint.

JENNY. I'm really sorry about that whole situation; I'll see that the bar is properly stocked in the future.

MAN. See that you do. Does the car parked outside belong to you?

JENNY. Yes.

MAN. Good, I'll need to borrow it. I have state lines to cross before I can safely seek medical attention.

JENNY. There isn't enough gas in the tank to get you out of the state.

MAN. Thank you for alerting me to that situation, I will remedy it. Where are the keys?

JENNY. In my purse.

MAN. And where is your purse?

JENNY. Just under the bar.

MAN. Is there anything else under the bar? Any object you could use to harm me?

JENNY. No.

MAN. Excuse me?

JENNY. No, sir. Only my purse and some bar supplies.

MAN. Wonderful, reach under slowly and hand it to me please.

JENNY. Just the keys?

MAN. Oh, I'll take the whole bag, thank you young lady. Now about that call you wanted to make—

JENNY. I would never do that, not anymore, not if you don't want me too.

MAN. I appreciate that. But go ahead and unplug the phone from the wall and hand it to me. I'd much prefer to cut the line, but present circumstances, you understand.

JENNY. Yes.

MAN. I think that covers everything. I appreciate everything you've done for me tonight, I really do. I hope you realize that in my own way I've actually already repaid you for you kindness.

JENNY. Yes, sir, I do. Thank you very much for coming in tonight, have a pleasant trip.

MAN. Thank you very much young lady. See how it pays to be polite?

END OF PLAY

B-MOVIE NIGHT:

EIGHT PLAYS OF PURE EXPLOITATION!

LARVA! by Sean Abley

BIRDS IN A CAGE by Kelly Goodman

COLD WAR by Greg Machlin

WORSTEST MOVIE EVER by Nathan Wellman

RAISE YOUR HAND... FROM THE DEAD! by Natalie Nicole Dressel

HOW TO BE ATTRACTIVE by Amy Seeley

SLAVES OF THE BEAN by Adam Hahn

LADY KILLERS by Megan Gogerty

SkyPilot Theatre Company in Los Angeles asked their Playwright's Wing to create a series of B-movie plays to be presented live on stage for a benefit performance. The result: Nuclear maggots, women in prison, murderous snowmen, disembodied body parts, and more filled the stage for their wildly popular "Night of the Living Fundraiser." And now Plays to Order is proud to present this collection of cinematic stageplays, ripe for exploitation by your own theater company, preferably on some dark and stormy night...

PLAYS
TO
ORDER

www.playstoorder.com

ALSO AVAILABLE

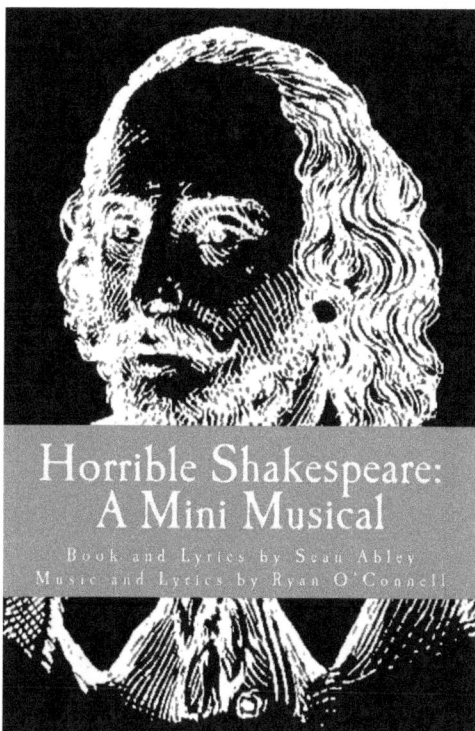

Musical
Short 30 minutes
Cast - 21 either

A student field trip to Shakespeare's Globe Theatre in London takes a horrible turn...literally! In this 30-minute musical, a nameless tour guide leads the students into the sub-sub-sub basement of the theater, which houses the Horrible Productions of Shakespeare's Plays Museum. Each exhibit magically transports the tour group into the world of a truly wretched production of some of Shakespeare's most famous works - "Romeo Mime vs. Clown Juliet," "Santa Hamlet," "Macbeth's Burgers," "Taming of the Real, Live Shrew" and "Twelfth Night of the Living Dead." This musical is perfect for festivals with time restrictions, in-class performances, or as one half of an evening of one-acts. Sheet music, demo tracks and performance karaoke tracks also available.

PLAYS
TO
ORDER
www.playstoorder.com